Cambridge Elements ≡

Elements in Intercultural Communication
edited by
Will Baker
University of Southampton
Troy McConachy
University of Warwick
Sonia Morán Panero
University of Southampton

TRANSLINGUAL DISCRIMINATION

Sender Dovchin
Curtin University

T0349752

CAMBRIDGE
UNIVERSITY PRESS

CAMBRIDGE
UNIVERSITY PRESS

Shaftesbury Road, Cambridge CB2 8EA, United Kingdom

One Liberty Plaza, 20th Floor, New York, NY 10006, USA

477 Williamstown Road, Port Melbourne, VIC 3207, Australia

314–321, 3rd Floor, Plot 3, Splendor Forum, Jasola District Centre, New Delhi – 110025, India

103 Penang Road, #05–06/07, Visioncrest Commercial, Singapore 238467

Cambridge University Press is part of Cambridge University Press & Assessment, a department of the University of Cambridge.

We share the University's mission to contribute to society through the pursuit of education, learning and research at the highest international levels of excellence.

www.cambridge.org
Information on this title: www.cambridge.org/9781009209731

DOI: 10.1017/9781009209748

First published 2022

A catalogue record for this publication is available from the British Library.

ISBN 978-1-009-20973-1 Paperback
ISSN 2752-5589 (online)
ISSN 2752-5570 (print)

Translingual Discrimination

Elements in Intercultural Communication

DOI: 10.1017/9781009209748
First published online: November 2022

Sender Dovchin
Curtin University

Author for correspondence: Sender Dovchin, sender.dovchin@curtin.edu.au

Abstract: Moving beyond two main concepts of interlingual and intralingual discrimination, this Element addresses the concept of translingual discrimination, which refers to inequality based on transnational migrants' specific linguistic and communicative repertoires that are (il)legitimised by the national order of things. Translingual discrimination adds intensity to transnational processes, with transnational migrants showing two main characteristics of exclusion – translingual name discrimination and its associated elements such as name stigma and name microaggression; and translingual English discrimination and its elements such as accentism, stereotyping, and hallucination. The accumulation of these characteristics of translingual discrimination causes negative emotionality in its victims, including foreign language anxiety and translingual inferiority complexes. Consequently, transnational migrants adopt coping strategies such as CV-whitening, renaming practices, purification, and ethnic evasion while searching for translingual safe spaces. The Element concludes with the social and pedagogical implications of translingual discrimination in relation to transnational migrants.

Keywords: translingualism, discrimination, English, migrants, transnationalism

ISBNs: 9781009209731 (PB), 9781009209748 (OC)
ISSNs: 2752-5589 (online), 2752-5570 (print)

Contents

1 Translingual Discrimination

1.1 Introduction

Widely reported across the Australian media was the death by suicide of Chinese national twenty-four-year-old Zhikai Liu, who had exhibited signs of undiagnosed mental ill health after moving to Australia to study at the University of Melbourne (SBS, 2019). Liu suffered from severe insomnia and started developing suicidal ideation. He refused to seek help for his suspected depression and later took his own life. One of the most severe triggers that worsened Liu's mental health was his insecurity and anxiety over his English language skills. As his sister described, her brother faced language barriers in Australia. He felt extremely anxious and depressed when he could not fully understand what was happening in his university classes while encountering the daily language used to communicate with people around him (Jamieson, 2018). According to the final report of the Victorian Coroner, Audrey Jamieson (2018), 'The investigation has identified that Mr Liu experienced suicidal ideation and demonstrated symptoms suggestive of depression, especially adjusting to his new environment, confronting language barriers and experiencing study difficulties at university.'

Zhikai Liu is just one of millions of 'transnational migrants' – mobile groups and individuals (e.g., moving groups, tourists, immigrants, refugees, guest workers, students, individuals, etc.) – within the current massive transnational flows of migration of people who are moving to new spaces (Appadurai, 1997). These transnational flows of human mobility can be regulated by the imaginations and fantasies of moving, or wanting to move to seek better social, educational, and financial opportunities (Appadurai, 1997). Yet, the major portion of these transnational migrants appears to be knocked back by the given realities of the 'national order of things' in the country of their settlement (Malkki, 1995a), or, as Löfgren has suggested, by an 'international cultural grammar of nationhood' (Löfgren, 1989, p. 21) – a set of general rules, traditions, and policies that are needed to form the nation-state. As Malkki (1995a, p. 516) notes in terms of movements of international refugees, '[j]ust as power secretes knowledge, the national order of things secretes displacement, as well as prescribed correctives for displacement'. Thus, the international refugee regime is, in fact, 'inseparable from this wider national order of things, this wider grammar' (Malkki, 1995a, p. 516).

In fact, when these transnational migrants are mobilised, they seem to be brought down to national systems based on the utopia of national sovereignty and the rigid national and domestic orders in many aspects of their lives (Hsu, 2020). In particular, the sociolinguistic practices and backgrounds of these transnational migrants seem to be some of the leading subversions of the national order of things (Dovchin & Dryden, 2022). This is exactly what happened to Zhikai Liu – a transnational migrant (more specifically, an international student from China to Australia) – who gravely suffered from an adverse impact of transnationalism, emerging specifically from the national 'language' order of things. This involved tension between the idealisation of standard Australian English (SAE) and the marginalisation of Zhikai's 'transnational' background English, which we also theoretically call 'translingual' English (Canagarajah, 2013) – the mobilisation of diverse semiotic resources and adaptation of different negotiation strategies to make meanings in English rather than focusing on fixed English grammar and its orderly linguistic systems.

This Element seeks to illustrate many of the real-world challenges of transnationalism by bringing out how transnational migrants can represent such a subversion of the national order of things in the domain of their language practices. As Malkki (1995b, p. 6) highlights,

> One of the most illuminating ways of getting at the categorical quality of the national order of things is to examine what happens when this order is challenged or subverted. Refugees can represent precisely such a subversion. They are an 'abomination' . . . produced and made meaningful by the categorical order itself, even as they are excluded from it.

In line with Malkki's point, I argue that when transnational migrants whose first language is, for example, not English move to an English-dominant host society, they subvert the rigid standard national language orders in the communicative aspects of their lives. More specifically, they suffer from translingual discrimination – language-based discrimination against transnational migrants, whose sociolinguistic backgrounds and linguistic practices are displaced, subverted, and challenged (Dovchin & Dryden, 2022). Translingual discrimination and its main effects, such as linguistic stratification, division, and prejudice, decrease the socio-emotional well-being and psychological and mental health of its victims as they seek to conform to the linguistic and cultural grammar of nationhood. We, as language educators, thus need to ask the following critical questions: In what ways do transnational migrants subvert and challenge the national order of language? To what extent do transnational migrants resist the order? Do they have any coping mechanisms? If so, how, what, and why? What emotional expressions result from encountering this order? How often and in what ways do they suffer from linguistic subversion? This Element, therefore, seeks to uncover how translingual discrimination is experienced by migrants, how they see themselves, and how we can understand their reflexive understanding of what translingual discrimination means to them.

1.2 Interlingual and Intralingual Discrimination

Decades of research on language discrimination in applied linguistics have been widely discussed in the main framework of linguistic human rights (LHR) (Blommaert, 2001a, 2001b; Makoni, 2012; Phillipson & Skutnabb-Kangas, 1995; Skutnabb-Kangas, 2000; Wee, 2005, 2011), foregrounding interlingual and intralingual discrimination (or interlanguage and intralanguage) as its two key concepts. Interlingual discrimination is mainly defined by the unequal hierarchical relationship between minority and hegemonic language groups at the level of inter-nations, where the minority groups cannot fully utilise their mother tongues or first languages in critical social, political, and educational participation. Particularly in postcolonial contexts, unequal ideologies and practices of interlingual discrimination are prevalent, while former colonial languages are still homogenising minority languages in critical social domains (Phillipson & Skutnabb-Kangas, 1995). The members of these minority groups are not able to fully exercise their linguistic rights to their mother tongues while also being denied the opportunity to become bi/multilingual in their mother tongues (Phillipson & Skutnabb-Kangas, 1995; Skutnabb-Kangas, 2000). A form of ethnic conflict, as a result, may lead to ethnic disintegration and conflicts, since minority languages are often linked to specific ethnic groups. Interlingual discrimination perspectives thereby resist discriminatory hegemonic linguistic practices, advocating for the revitalisation of minority languages and the development of compulsory conventions on linguistic human rights. For example, previous studies show the oppression of minority languages, which has been widespread in many former colonies. The French language has been maintained in parts of Africa, while national, ethnic, or minority languages were violated and subverted (Salhi, 2002). English has been and continues to be an imperialistic language, as there is still massive unequal linguistic power between English and other global languages. Anglophone nations, for example, use English to suppress other non-English-speaking nations around the world (Phillipson, 1992, 2010). Intralingual discrimination has been evident in situations such as immigrant children being subjected to corporal punishment for the 'crime' of speaking their mother tongue in the context of the Celtic languages in Britain or France, or Sami in Scandinavia. The same discrimination was also apparent in the Europeanised countries of the Americas and Australasia, and in colonial Africa. The same applies to the exclusion of the Kurdish language in Turkey, while the Turkish language is promoted as the standard language (Phillipson & Skutnabb-Kangas, 1995).

While the concept of interlingual discrimination has strongly advocated for the critical significance of minority language rights, continually striking a note of caution towards the unequal power relations between minority and hegemonic languages at the level of inter-nations and states, it also closes an investigation of the complexity of intra-groups' sociolinguistic realities (Blommaert, 2001a, 2001b). The account of interlingual discrimination, as a result, has been criticised by certain scholars for reducing inequality to interlanguage diversity at the level of inter-nations, particularly constraining its understanding only on 'named languages' that are accepted by the national order of things. As Blommaert (2001a, p. 135) points out, the main flaw in interlingual discrimination consists of 'Diversity and inequality within particular units conventionally called "language" is not treated (there is cursory mention of it, but it remains undeveloped). What is at stake is the difference between, e.g., "French" and "Berber", "English" and "Swahili", "Dutch" and "French": things that have a name.' In other words, language discrimination, with its simple 'hegemonic–minority' model, is reduced to conflicts between standard language categories. Its diversion from internal inequalities within a nation presupposes the existence of a 'language community' since it assumes that 'the promotion of the mother tongue is the best way to ensure the protection of speakers' socio-economic interests' (Wee, 2005, p. 49). The account of interlingual discrimination, therefore, leads to the idea that the battlefield of linguistic discrimination is constructed by nations, each identified by a language, and nations are effectively defined as ethnolinguistic groups (Blommaert, 2001a). Nevertheless, the association of 'language' with 'named languages' could be highly problematic because there is also a massive inequality internally embedded within those particular 'named languages'.

While the term 'interlingual discrimination' is not necessarily obsolescent and still has applications in the context of inter-nation linguistic power struggles in several ways, the concept of intralanguage or intralingual discrimination has instead been proposed as a better candidate to grasp internal or intra-group linguistic inequalities (Blommaert, 2001a, 2001b; Makoni, 2012; Wee, 2005, 2011). To understand language discrimination, it is essential to understand internal language inequalities, 'the situation where speakers themselves exercise control over their language, deciding what languages are, and what they may mean' (Stroud, 2001, p. 353). While interlingual discrimination suggests that minority languages are becoming the victims of former colonial language homogenisation, here we get the other side of the coin, the intralingual position, focusing on the implications of the internal variations within each language. If an intralingual variation is accepted as a potential source of discrimination, then speakers of non-standard varieties of the standard language can claim to be the victims of discrimination as they are judged to be less acceptable than their standard-using counterparts (Makoni, 2012). Intralingual discrimination is, as Wee (2005, p. 54) notes, 'less often linked to distinct ethnic identities', and is more likely to lead to 'social' rather than 'ethnic' conflicts, 'where speakers of the non-standard variety are judged to be less sophisticated or less respectable than their standard-speaking counterparts'. The tension between the standard form associated with an institutional setting such as school and the degrading of a non-standard variety associated with informal settings such as home may mean that language users often collude in their own intralingual discrimination (Wee, 2011). Users of Singaporean English (Singlish) are, for example, potentially discriminated against due to a language policy that promotes standard English in Singapore while devaluing other language varieties such as Singlish (Wee, 2011). The controversy regarding which variety to use in formal domains also surfaces in parts of Africa (Makoni, 2012), where, for example, an issue before the court was raised by a mother whose son was being taught a wrong variety of isiZulu, 'kitchen (isi)Zulu', which was claimed to have adversely affected her son's development of proficiency in isiZulu. A similar example is also apparent in Mongolia, where the non-standard Mongolian dialects, accents, and pronunciations practised mainly in the remote or rural regions can be marginalised by the mainstream urban population (Dovchin, 2018). Intralingual discrimination is, therefore, mainly contested within an in-group space, where the speakers of a non-standard variety may endure resistance even from their fellow speakers within the same linguistic and cultural group (Blommaert, 2001a).

While a canonical view of intralingual discrimination is defined by the understanding that speakers are discriminated against based on certain in-group linguistic variations and internal language sub-varieties, investigating intralingual discrimination may also involve a host of exclusions (Dovchin & Dryden, 2022). The core belief of intralingual discrimination raises questions about whether it sufficiently addresses the superdiverse linguistic differentiation beyond intra-groups and its complex transnational and transcultural interconnection with other social, ethnic, racial, gender, technological, political, economic, and ideological factors. Its focus is on particular group-specific and in-group linguistic community rights predicated on notions of intra-group discrimination and inequality. It is, for example, still centred around nationally defined or 'standardised' sub-varieties such as Singlish, within the same linguistic community nation such as Singapore. The core linguistic battlefield is between the standard and non-standard varieties within the same linguistic community nation, still aiming towards the central grammar and lexicon of sub-varieties of the dominant language, which is what makes Singlish, for example, still English, with English characterised by various grammatical shifts, new lexical items, and different pragmatic and phonological features.

Indeed, language discrimination may also occur within, beyond, and across intra-groups because someone who is intralingually discriminated against in one context may be included and validated in another, depending on which aspects of an individual's identity are engaged by that time and space (Dick, 2011). Speakers of Singlish, for example, are not necessarily subject to the disadvantages of intralanguage discrimination because their Singlish can also be appreciated when they move beyond Singaporean contexts, where these varieties are, for example, accepted or even celebrated. A young Mongolian man who learned his English based primarily on African-American English vernacular from hip hop music in Mongolia was largely admired by his peers for using 'cool English' or 'American English' in Mongolia. Yet, when he moved to Australia, his English was discriminated against as 'accented' and 'not up to standard' (Dovchin, 2018).

Intralingual discrimination, centred on nationally defined or 'standardised' sub-varieties, lacks adequacy to deal with other numerous linguistic possibilities and contexts in current transnational conditions. Its attempt to understand the discrimination against the 'systematised' substandard national variants tends to leave out many other new, superdiverse, hybrid forms of transnational linguistic potentials (Dovchin & Dryden, 2022). Makoni (2014, p. 28, for example, points out the intralingual discrimination framework does not address 'gendered forms of language discrimination, thereby underscoring the complexity of the notions of language and "group" on which LHR is anchored, including the complex interconnectedness of cultural communicative practices and power'. This framework, therefore, must consider socially and discursively constructed transnational group relations that may reflect diverse forms of language discrimination.

Interlingual discrimination does not take us far enough and remains an exclusionary paradigm: just as Blommaert (2001a, 2001b) has argued that the concept of interlingual discrimination may do little more than pluralise monolingual discrimination between named inter-languages, so I am suggesting that the concept of intralingual discrimination does little more than to pluralise the discrimination between the standard and 'named' sub-varieties of those same language groups. This framework, therefore, must consider socially and discursively constructed transnational groups, who are constantly displaced or re-placed; de-territorialised or re-territorialised in this current globalised world, covering diverse and complex layered forms of language discrimination. Intralingual discrimination, therefore, cannot do justice to those 'other' kaleidoscopic (Pennycook, 2007, 2008), vernacular, and pidgin (Mufwene, 2002), or emergent transidiomatic practices (Jacquemet, 2013), defined by one's transnational movement in Appadurai's (1997) vision of globalisation.

1.3 Translingual Discrimination

Moving away from the two dominant visions of interlingual and intralingual discrimination, I locate the idea of language discrimination in the space of re-placed and displaced transnational migrants within a more complex alternative position that I call 'translingual discrimination' (Dovchin & Dryden, 2022). As transnational migrants start moving to new spaces for more opportunities, they also retain the imprint of both their countries of origin and of settlement, 'driven by diverse goals, serving different needs of the nation-state, and equipped with varying levels of capital' (Darvin & Norton, 2014, p. 113). Transnational migrants, per Bhabha's (1994) 'third space', and their movements allow for a superdiversity of forms of contact and communication that are available in a range of transnational communicative resources, codes, modes, styles, and repertoires (Hawkins & Mori, 2018). The sociolinguistic movements of these transnational migrants are often treated as emergent, constantly being re-constructed by the communicative dynamics of their participants (Li, 2018). As a result, new terminologies, such as the users of 'translingual' (Canagarajah, 2018; Lee, 2022; J. Lee, 2017), 'translanguaging' (Fang & Liu, 2020), 'transi-diomatic' (Jacquemet, 2013), 'transglossic' (Sultana et al., 2015), 'tranßcripting' (Li & Zhu, 2019), and 'transgrammaring' (Barrett, 2019, 2020) practices are recognised by applied linguists, inclusive of a 'trans- turn' to fully capture the linguistic and communicative complexity of these trans-national migrants. The fundamental tenet of this 'trans- turn' problematises the traditional bi/multilingual view of language to separate linguistic categories through bounded language categories. Instead, it advocates for the shifting between and across linguistic and semiotic repertoires, presenting on-the-spot and embryonic negotiation of fluid resources for meaning-making (Lee & Dovchin, 2019). Transnational migrants are actively engaged with the continual process of semiotic mobility across time and space, and displacement from and replacement into a newer context while resemioticising (Tebaldi, 2020) and relocalising available resources (Tankosić & Dovchin, 2022). The essential importance is on language users' 'fluid and creative adaptation of a wide array of semiotic resources' and language as 'a product of their sociohistorical trajectories through a multitude of interactions across space and time' (Hawkins & Mori, 2018, pp. 2–3).

Meanwhile, this very idea of 'trans-' movement in applied linguistics has long been outshone by the translingual practices and experiences of 'playfulness' (Li et al., 2020; Tai & Li, 2021) of its participants, mediated mainly by digital communication (Li & Zhu, 2019), popular culture (Dovchin et al., 2017), social media (Schreiber, 2015), and other types of youth cultures (Rampton et al., 2019). Translingual practices are frequently understood as linguistically creative (Bradley et al., 2018) and innovative (Lee & Dovchin, 2019) while enjoying full participation in translingual communication in its all-fantastic dimensions – the sounds, the shapes, the unfamiliar combinations, and the odd grammatical structures (Kramsch, 2006). The playfulness in trans-perspectives celebrates translingual users' creativity, innovation, and positivity, focusing on vivacity and energy. This trend is, of course, associated with the fact that one's translingual register is intensely connected with a celebration of re-becoming, changing, re-transforming, re-creating, and renewal (Dovchin et al., 2017), privileging the kind of 'heterodox language mixing that features in everyday recreation on the ground' (Rampton et al., 2019, p. 648). 'Playful talk' is becoming popular in trans- perspectives. It entails a 'wide range of verbal activities and routines, including teasing, joking, humour, verbal play, parody, music making, chanting that can emerge in learners' talk' (Lytra, 2008, p. 185) while allowing users to bring and incorporate various resources into their daily communicative repertoires. These linguistic resources are often multimodal (e.g., drawings, arts, links, and emojis), expressive (e.g., word choice, laughter, gesture, voice tone), and include 'playful naughtiness' (Creese & Blackledge, 2010, p. 111) through 'pleasure of doing things differently' (Pennycook, 2007, pp. 41–2) to create alternative linguistic, cultural, and identity practices (Sayer, 2013).

Nevertheless, not all linguistically trans- practices and encounters are 'playful' because the sociolinguistic realities of transnational migrants can also be predominantly overshadowed by precarity, disparity, racism, and inequality orchestrated by the national order of things in the settlement society (Dovchin, 2021). The mobility of transnational migrants, which may, in fact, intensely feed the 'discrimination', has been reductively represented in the studies of trans- perspectives, while the impact of translingual playfulness has been discussed considerably. It is apparent that transnational migrants are playfully involved with different types of trans- practices, but it is not at all clear to what extent, how, and why particular local constraints either limit or expand one's translingual practices. Transnational migrants can be linguistically playful, but they are also deeply embedded in local economies of order and disparity (Dovchin, 2021). How do we, for example, understand when a young Mongolian migrant woman's 'Mongolian-sounding English accent' may create a 'playful' interaction with her Australian interlocutors while they also tease her for having a 'sexy' accent? Perhaps an 'English accent' spoken by a Mongolian person may sound playful to some English users. However, from the perspective of this young Mongolian woman, it is neither playful nor joyful to be teased for her accent. In other words, the contemporary theorisation of trans- perspectives does not sufficiently interrogate the disparity and discrimination experienced by its users, romanticising the creativity of language without sufficiently interrogating injustices involving race, ethnicity, gender, and socio-economic realities (Kubota, 2015). Research on global Englishes (Jenkins, 2007; Jenkins & Mauranen, 2019; Tupas & Rubdy, 2015) similarly reminds us that current approaches towards hybrid English brush aside inequalities that mediate relations between English users since they have been seduced into celebrating hybrid English but overlook the massive inequities sustained by the different usages of English today (cf. Milroy & Milroy, 2012). This type of inequality is apparent, for example, in academic contexts, where British universities expect British standard English, which also goes for American English and North American universities (Jenkins & Mauranen, 2019).

The conceptual understanding of translingual discrimination thus aims to fill this critical research gap in existing trans- theories, urging a more vital need to acknowledge one of its most overlooked characteristics – linguistic discrimination experienced by so-called playful and creative translingual users and migrants. The concept of translingual discrimination thereby points to the critical issues between language and inequality, innovating the analytic potential of applied linguistic theories by taking concepts such as linguistic racism (Corona & Block, 2020; Dovchin, 2020a), unequal Englishes (Tupas & Rubdy, 2015), raciolinguistics (Rosa & Flores, 2017), and linguicism (Skutnabb-Kangas, 2015) seriously. The main ethos of these concepts is to reveal the unequal power relationship between ideologies and practices such as so-called native or non-native, first or second language users (Kumaravadivelu, 2016). The focus is on the central role that language plays in the enduring relevance of race/racism, institutional/interpersonal discrimination in the lives of migrants, racialised or ethnic minorities in the highly diverse transnational host societies of the twenty-first century, and what it means to speak or communicate as people with transnational identities. It further examines how an individual's basic human rights are violated, and how they are deprived of education, employment, health, and social opportunities, based on their use of language (Dovchin, 2020a). Integrating these main arguments in current trans- perspectives will break new ground by disclosing the sociolinguistic reality that it is not always applicable to celebrate translingual playfulness without fully acknowledging ongoing, often deeply entrenched, local constraints. It is almost impossible to develop a thorough analysis of people's apparent translingual choices without acknowledging how ongoing communication is always associated with the existing social experiences of those making these choices. Hence, the idea of translingual discrimination may become helpful in understanding the relationships among transnational linguistic practices, dominant ideologies, and structural inequalities.

So, what is translingual discrimination? The concept of translingual discrimination refers to the ideologies and practices that produce unequal linguistic power relationships between the transnational migrant-background language users and the majority population from the host society, focusing on the central role that language plays in the enduring relevance of discrimination, disparity, and exclusion in the lives of transnational migrants. Translingual discrimination is language-based discrimination against transnational migrants in the host society, whose sociolinguistic backgrounds and linguistic practices are displaced, subverted, and challenged. As transnational migrants operate in different spaces, they are often positioned in multiple different and unequal settings as their particular sociolinguistic backgrounds and the past experiences they bring with them are assigned different national values and standards that may eventually cause them to become subject to discrimination in their countries of settlement. Blommaert's (2010) idea of an 'order of indexicality' is essential here for translingual discrimination since 'indexicality', in Blommaert's vision (2010, p. 38), as 'registers', 'social categories', and 'recognisable semiotic emblems' for groups and individuals, is ordered in hierarchies of value in different contexts. As Blommaert (2010, p. 38) describes, those orders of indexicalities may operate within 'large stratified complexes in which some forms of semiosis are systematically perceived as valuable', while others are 'less valuable and some are not taken into account at all'. Then, all are subject to 'rules of access and regulations as to circulation'. From this perspective, the concept of translingual discrimination refers to the different orders of indexicality with which transnational migrants' sociolinguistic practices and backgrounds are embedded, as some forms of translingual indexicality can be deemed as legitimate, while others can be seen as less valued. In translingual discrimination, some indexicality is not accepted at all, while all are subject to systemic orders of standardisation and nativisation as to circulation by the national political and socio-cultural context (Lippi-Green, 2011). Standard monolingual national language ideologies are primarily enforced on how transnationals communicate, while their translingual backgrounds only gain importance when others validate or legitimise them (Flores & Rosa, 2015; Foo & Tan, 2019). What may be a gain or advantage in one context can be a total loss in another. The English spoken or used by an upper-middle-class person in Mongolia, for example, is unlikely to be validated as upper-middle-class quality in London or Oxford. What happens to transnational migrants in their communication in the host society becomes less stable than what would occur in their home environment.

This view of the orders of indexicality embedded within translingual discrimination also reminds us of Goffman's (1963, p. 6) classic work on 'interaction order' – 'individuals are socially situated, and situate themselves, through language, in distinctive ways that are shaped by a shared focus and identification of their interlocutor'. From this view, translingual interaction orders may become a recipe for discrimination because interlocutors can make a judgement of one another – not only how they speak or communicate, but also by the intersectionality of their outer 'appearance, tone of voice, mention of name, or other person-differentiating device' (Goffman 1963, p. 3). It only takes, however, 'a slight deviation' from habitual or routine practice to send an individual on the receiving end into 'interpretive overdrive', as they might start to judge the situation 'when a sound, a word, a grammatical pattern, a discourse move or bodily movement does not quite fit' (Blommaert & Rampton, 2011, p. 12). This minor deviation from the norms of indexicality may affect people's judgement in perceiving what is (il)legitimate in the 'situated indexical interpretations that they bring to bear ("good" or "bad", "right" or "wrong", "art" or "error", "call it out", or "let it pass", "indicative or typical of this or that")' (Blommaert & Rampton, 2011, p. 12).

To sum up, the concept of translingual discrimination refers to linguistic inequality orchestrated by the national order of things, and linguistic and communicative 'orders of indexicality', in which transnational migrants' specific linguistic and communicative registers and sociolinguistic backgrounds are often rejected as soon as they mobilise in the current transnational movement (Appadurai, 1997; Dovchin, 2018). As Dovchin and Dryden (2022, p. 369) note, '[e]very translingual indexicality is susceptible to a systemic pattern of authority, of control and evaluation, while concurrently shaping modes of linguistic inclusion and exclusion, and linguistic privileging and marginalisation'. Translingual discrimination thus points out critical aspects of power and inequality, where some linguistic registers that are considered as 'good', 'acceptable', or 'legitimate' may not be good enough in other contexts. Translingual discrimination is, therefore, the main product of unequal power relations: it stratifies the registers and indexicality of transnational migrants, diminishing their power in the extent of language as they encounter a new form of linguistic discrimination that could potentially project the intersectionality of racial, ethnic, cultural, and other discriminatory beliefs and practices.

The concept of translingual discrimination, therefore, will ask new critical questions: In what ways and how do transnational migrants subvert and challenge language-based discrimination? To what extent do transnational migrants resist linguistic discrimination? How do we uncover transnational migrants' metalinguistic awareness through their own linguistic and communicative repertoires? And how do these transnational migrants discursively unpack what translingual discrimination means to them? In what ways and how do transnational migrants subvert and challenge the national order of language? To what extent do transnational migrants resist this order? Do they have any coping mechanisms? If so, how, what, and why? What emotional expressions result from encountering this order? How often and in what ways do they suffer from linguistic subversion? In order to better understand the concept of translingual discrimination, the qualitative research methodology of linguistic ethnography (LE) (see section 1.5) will be the main line of inquiry in this Element, which investigates human linguistic and communicative attitudes, behaviours, activities, and practices formulated by and within their own socio-cultural, ethnolinguistic, and social environments (Blommaert & Dong, 2010; Blommaert & Rampton, 2011).

1.4 The Elements of Translingual Discrimination

In this Element, translingual discrimination will be further discussed, including multiple elements embedded within its main characteristics, such as translingual name discrimination (section 2), translingual English discrimination (section 3), and translingual inferiority complexes (section 4). In section 2, one of the primary instances of translingual discrimination is discussed – translingual name discrimination, in which the transnational migrants' social and economic opportunities are instantly subverted and their intrinsic qualities and skills are immediately reduced based on their birth name (Dovchin & Dryden, 2022). Translingual name stigma refers to a collective stigma based on imaginary negative attributes associated with transnational migrants' birth names, as the name carriers can be stereotyped as less skilled than the normatively named majority irrespective of their actual intrinsic skills. Translingual name microaggression refers to the micro and subtle form of name discrimination against migrants' birth names, including mispronunciation, misspelling, misunderstanding, misgendering, mocking, or failing to remember the migrants' birth names. To resist these elements, many transnational migrants downplay their ethno-racial clues to make it easier for English eyes by adopting a coping strategy of CV-whitening – Anglicising their names or any other ethnic clues in their CVs. Migrants also adopt the strategy of renaming practices that fit English mouths to pronounce and English ears to hear.

In section 3, 'Translingual English Discrimination', the ideologies and practices that may exclude or marginalise transnational migrants based on their usage, proficiency, and practices of English – judged against the 'standard' form of English – will be discussed. The element of translingual English accentism refers to practices that marginalise and contest transnational migrants' biographical English accents against other standard-English accents Dovchin & Dryden (2022). The element of translingual English stereotyping and hallucination refers to practices in which English users with transnational migrant backgrounds are often stereotyped as having low proficiency in English regardless of their actual fluent English skills, primarily due to how they look. To resist these elements, transnational migrants adopt coping strategies by 'purifying' their biographical accent – the constant effort of eliminating their accent while seeking to acquire a new standard accent and adopting the strategy of ethnic evasion, as they develop no interest in their heritage language and culture and avoid socialising with their own ethnic groups.

In section 4, how and to what extent transnational migrants suffer from negative emotionality traits that are caused by the accumulation of elements of translingual discrimination will be discussed. 'Foreign language anxiety' – the feeling of anxiety, fear, and tension specifically associated with foreign language communication contexts – is common among transnational migrants. 'Translingual inferiority complexes' refer to the harmful psychological, emotional, and physical damage inflicted on the victims of translingual discrimination, which leads not only to the psychological and emotional traits of self-marginalisation, self-vindication, loss of social belonging and self-confidence, depression, and social withdrawal, but also physical damage such as eating disorders, drug abuse, and self-harm. Consequently, transnational migrants adopt a coping strategy by creating 'translingual safe spaces' – physical or social spaces that enable transnational migrants to get together and discuss their barriers and challenges, employing their full linguistic repertoires without regard for watchful adherence to the socially and politically defined boundaries of the standard language.

In the concluding section 5, I outline critical social and pedagogical implications emerging from translingual discrimination and its elements. While it is far too easy to lament translingual discrimination, the final social and pedagogical implications that are highlighted are graver than that. It is ultimately about the discrepancies between the rigid national order of things for transnational migrants and spaces where many migrants no longer correspond to the classifications of such orders. We, as language educators, therefore need to consider critical social and educational implications in order to raise the intercultural awareness of educators, policymakers, and the mainstream population.

1.5 Methodological Notes: Linguistic Ethnography

The study in this Element was conducted with regulations for ethical research approved by the Human Research Ethics Office, Curtin University, based on two larger studies, which overall investigated the language practices of 160 English as an Additional Language (EAL) background transnational migrants living in Western Australia (WA) in the period from August 2018 until May 2022. Most participants who participated in this research were culturally and linguistically diverse background transnational migrants from the Global South, including countries such as Mongolia, Ukraine, China, Russia, Korea, Syria, Somalia, Philippines, Vietnam, Japan, Colombia, India, Pakistan, and Bangladesh, who had lived in Australia between six months and fifteen years. Eighty per cent of the participants were women aged between eighteen and fifty-five, with the other 20 per cent being men aged between eighteen and fifty (see Appendix 1). Before data collection, all participants received a participant information sheet, a consent form, and a project leaflet in a physical or a digital form. As most participants in the study were the users of EAL, a detailed explanation adapted to their level of English proficiency or equivalent translated version in their first language was provided to ensure a complete understanding of the research aims and questions. Even though there were no foreseeable risks or inconveniences from the research project, all participants were still provided contact information for counselling services if the project impacted their psychological well-being or mental health. Participation in the research was voluntary, allowing participants to withdraw at any stage of the research project. All participants' names, some institutions, and some physical locations have been given pseudonyms to ensure anonymity.

The data were collected and analysed using the qualitative research method-ology of linguistic ethnography, which investigates human linguistic and com-municative attitudes, behaviours, activities, and practices influenced by and within their own socio-cultural, ethnolinguistic, and social environments (Blommaert & Dong, 2010; Blommaert & Rampton, 2011). As a qualitative ethnographic inquiry, it is primarily defined by a portrayal of culture practised by people in a certain space and at a certain time, which encompasses the study, observation, illustration, and description of human practices, human identities, and all aspects of their lives in their everyday life settings (Pérez-Milans, 2015). Adding 'linguistics' into 'ethnography' complements the study of LE, as its interpretation has a significant role in understanding human linguistic practices from ethnographic perspectives (Copland & Creese, 2015). The investigation of diverse communities allows a linguistic ethnographer to integrate themselves and become a part of people's linguistic practices and language experiences, which enables the discovery of new research questions and paradigms, and the exploration of linguistic aspects of human practices (Shah, 2017). LE allows the ethnographer to become the observer, while participants become the main actors in their story, giving their own thoughts and perspectives of the world and society around them, thus providing insights about their role in interactions within broader social structures (Dovchin, 2019a, 2020b, 2021). It also sets up possibilities for constant and extended company between the ethnographer and the key participants through natural interactions, making the ethnographers' interpretations more realistic as both parties are often co-invested in communication, creating more meaningful relationships and in-depth insights into participants' thoughts and actions (Shaw et al., 2015).

Open ethnographic observation (OEO) is one of the main methods of LE. OEO is primarily used to document the sociolinguistic practices of transnational migrants by observing them as they go about their everyday lives, and entails documentation through field notes of multiple observations, on-the-spot communication, and reflections that are experienced by the ethnographer at the site of the investigation (Copland & Creese, 2015). OEO further sets up possibilities for informal discussions, interactions, and interviews, making the ethnographers' interpretations more accurate and reliable as they can create more meaningful relationships with the participants. It further allows for the formation of mutual partnerships, or 'discursive shadowing' (Dewilde & Creese, 2016), in which the ethnographer and the participants are often co-invested and collaborate in the dialogues.

In terms of the researcher's positionality, I shared a similar ethnic and sociolinguistic (Mongolian) background with some participants from Mongolia. I also shared a similar lived experience with most of these research participants as a transnational migrant from the Global South, a user of English as an additional language, and someone living and working in Australia as a country of settlement. I moved to Australia from Mongolia to undertake my postgraduate degrees and ended up working at Curtin University a few years after my graduation. I also worked as an associate professor in Japan for about year and a half before I started working at Curtin University. This experience offered me an insightful perspective to better understand how the research participants reacted to and interacted with translingual discrimination, and why and in what ways they acted in challenging situations. Nevertheless, I positioned myself as both insider and outsider researcher to avoid the risk of being too familiar with the context. As a linguistic ethnographer, I played multiple roles: observer, researcher, interlocutor, and peer. Some of these roles were either mutually exclusive or complemented one another at different times. Maintaining these multiple roles was challenging as a researcher, but it also allowed valuable, in-depth insights (Dewilde & Creese, 2016).

All data examples used in this Element were retrieved from audio recordings and fieldwork written notes of semi-structured interviews, focus group discussions, follow-up discussions, and natural or informal interactions with research participants during OEO. Most of the time, the researcher spent between one and two hours with the participants, doing as many activities as possible together, such as cooking, shopping, hiking, visiting cafes, or attending the library. After spending considerable time together, the participants were informed about the beginning of the audio-recording, and the main questions were raised to understand what participants' everyday sociolinguistic practice would look like (Dovchin, 2021). Most of the audio recordings were between sixty and ninety minutes, primarily in English. However, some participants had opportunities to use their first languages, such as Mongolian, Russian, Korean, Chinese, and Ukrainian. If the data records were not in English, they were translated from the source language into English by the researchers and interpreters. All non-English source texts expressed in these different languages used in this Element were Romanised based on ISO standards for transliterations of Romanisations (www.iso.org/iso/home.html). The main ethos of the research questions was primarily geared towards these transnationals' main linguistic and communicative challenges of living in Australia as a migrant, their linguistic choices, and barriers resulting from their sociolinguistic background as transnational migrants. In that way, participants gained the opportunity to share their experiences and narratives as experienced by them, as well as to offer their own meta-reflections on matters recognised by myself as a researcher.

To ensure rigorous and accurate analysis, the data collected from LE enabled us to cross-examine further the findings, where we used two different methods (deductive codes/inductive codes) to verify the findings (Dovchin, 2020b, 2021). The cross-examination tracked both deductive codes concerning research questions and inductive codes regarding the research participants' reflections. It also enabled verification and editing of text transcripts to ensure the accuracy of the communication, while the final transcribed and coded text, which was exported from Trint (an automated transcription software program) (Dovchin, 2020b, 2021). After completing data coding, data extracts from interactions were analysed from the perspective of what the research participants told us (content) (Dryden & Dovchin, 2021). The data cross-examination illustrated that all participants had experienced self-reported translingual discrimination in explicit and implicit ways in varied contexts in Australia, from informal to formal settings (Tankosić & Dovchin, 2021). Note, however, that not every single data record gathered during OEO was used in this Element, as including every participant's voice proved impossible due to the sheer amount of content. Nevertheless, all data were double cross-examined through deductive/inductive codes, which disclosed the main thematic analysis and allowed for the categorisation of data into sets of main themes such as translingual name discrimination, translingual English discrimination, and translingual discrimination and emotionality. These were then categorised for their content similarities and differences for different sections in this Element.

2 Translingual Name Discrimination

2.1 Translingual Name Discrimination

'What's in a name? That which we call a rose by any other name would smell just as sweet' (Olson, 2020, p. 43). When William Shakespeare uses this line in his play *Romeo and Juliet*, he indicates that the naming of someone is as arbitrary as it can get compared to one's intrinsic qualities. It seems Shakespeare was right. Transnational migrants' intrinsic qualities are often discounted in their country of settlement because of a simple arbitrary reason – how their name sounds different, looks odd, or is pronounced awkwardly according to the perceptions of first-language English speakers. Many transnational migrants strive to live up to their birth names (Dovchin & Dryden, 2022). One's birth name carries crucial symbolic meaning in terms of one's cultural, ethnic, linguistic, and familial significance as it connects a person's cultural heritage to his/her roots, ancestors, home country, or ethnic group (Kohli & Solórzano, 2012). However, because names are so unambiguous and basic to every individual everywhere, they are often taken for granted and not given the theoretical and analytical scrutiny that they deserve in applied linguistics. Practices of naming or names are, according to Palsson (2014, p. 618), 'not only key elements of identification and personhood, embodied in the biosocial habitus much like other biomarkers' but they also 'situate people in genealogies, social networks, and states'. Names are identities, and names are histories.

Nevertheless, Palsson also reminds us that names not only 'specify and individualise their bearers' (2014, p. 619) but also, following Foucault's (1988) understanding of 'technologies of the self", serve 'as means of domination and empowerment, facilitating collective action, surveillance, and subjugation – exclusion as well as belonging' (Palsson, 2014, p. 619). As Palsson (2014, pp. 618–19) suggests, 'Clashes … between different traditions and practices of naming, especially in the context of slavery and empires, illuminate with striking clarity the relevance of names as technologies of exclusion, subjugation, and belonging'. This warning by Palsson poses several questions: To what extent do naming practices and names represent translingual discrimination in the broadest sense, as they become the primary cause of exclusion, subjugation, and a sense of non-belonging? What kinds of roles do names play in the lived experiences of transnational migrants? Why would transnational migrants adopt new names?

Drawing on transnational migrants' names and naming practices in the context of Australia, this section discusses one of the primary and most prominent instances of translingual discrimination – translingual name discrimination – where transnational migrants' social and economic opportunities are instantly disqualified, and their intrinsic qualities and skills are immediately discounted, often on the basis of the flimsiest of evidence – that is, one's birth name (Dovchin & Dryden, 2022). Because the names and naming practices of transnational migrants may identify their ethnic, linguistic, and cultural identities, they may often deviate from the normative naming traditions in the host society, which may allow instant misjudgement and stereotyping (Oreopoulos, 2011). Transnational migrants' birth names are never judged in separation from their owners. These names carry pre-fixed negative stigmas and bring into question their owners' intelligence, skills, linguistic fluency, and education. As a result, migrants often seek to downplay their ethno-racial signifiers 'to make it easier for "English" ears and eyes, as their personal experiences have taught them that any effort to use their birth name from coffee orders (e.g., all-Australian names that are easy to scribble on the side of a coffee cup) to job or housing applications' is faced with some sort of misjudgement (Dovchin & Dryden, 2022, p. 371). Some of the most common ideologies and practices of translingual name discrimination – translingual name stigma and translingual name microaggressions, and their associated coping strategies such as CV-whitening (Kang et al, 2016) and renaming practices (Kohli & Solórzano, 2012) – will be discussed in this section.

2.2 Translingual Name Stigma

In his classic work, Goffman (1963) pointed out that being a racial minority can instigate a form of tribal stigma – a collective stigma based on imagined or imaginary attributes associated with certain racial groups. Translingual name stigma, following the idea of tribal stigma, refers to a collective stigma based on imagined or imaginary attributes associated with transnational migrants' birth names. The birth name of transnational migrants may cause negative stigmas about its name carriers as less skilled, less educated, or less capable than the normative majority, irrespective of their actual social, educational, and linguistic backgrounds and skills (Dovchin & Dryden, 2022). This, in turn, may lead to 'discrimination, through which we effectively, if often unthinkingly, reduce [a person's] life chances' (Goffman, 1963, p. 5).

Translingual name stigma is primarily found in the initial hiring process of recruitment when the candidate's CV is examined (Oreopoulos, 2011), which is also consistent with a study conducted by the International Labour Office (Allasino et al., 2004). Riach and Rich's (2002) study found that nearly 90 per cent of the total level of ethnic discrimination occurs in the initial employment stage because it is easier for employers not to interview potential employees rather than fire them later (Riach & Rich, 2002). In one experimental (correspondence test) study, the researchers randomly assigned typical White-sounding and ethnic-sounding names to two similar fictitious CVs (Oreopoulos, 2011). The results indicated that CVs containing ethnic indications, such as distinctively ethnic-sounding African American or Asian names, led to much fewer call-backs than CVs without any such clues. Those with White- or English-sounding names received interview requests 40 per cent more often than applicants with, for example, Chinese, Indian, or Pakistani names (Oreopoulos, 2011). Similarly, Edo et al.'s (2019) study investigates the importance of ethnic homophily in the hiring discrimination process in France, in which they used three different kinds of ethnic identification: French sounding names, North African sounding names, and 'foreign' sounding names with no clear ethnic association. All non-French applicants were equally discriminated against when compared to French sounding names, and French-named applicants were more likely to receive a call-back. The evidence of a name discriminatory pattern in the context of virtual reference services of libraries, which allows users to connect easily with librarians online, was also apparent in the study by Shachaf and Horowitz (2006). While librarians answer thousands of questions every day over the Internet, it was revealed that they were more likely to ignore or respond more slowly to the requests of Arabic and African American usernames than White, Christian, or Jewish usernames. The librarians also put less time and effort into their replies. They did not adhere to professional guidelines regarding courtesy and politeness to the same degree as when responding to White, Christian, or Jewish usernames. This outcome is reiterated by Tonin's (2018) study of public services in the US, in which almost 5,000 emails were sent to public libraries and other public services by unaffiliated users. The emails signed by African American-sounding names were 4 per cent less likely to receive a response from library services than those signed by White-sounding names, and 5 per cent less likely to be addressed by name or receive a greeting from the library service. African American-sounding names received lower levels of courtesy and a lower total response rate than White-sounding names, indicating naming stigma based purely on the perceived ethnicity or race of the sender (Tonin, 2018). Overall, these studies, when viewed cumulatively, suggest considerable employer discrimination against applicants with ethnic names.

Similarly, one of the most common forms of translingual name stigma was evidenced in the initial hiring process of employment in this study. Many research participants (to be more specific, transnational migrants with ethnic names) revealed that they received no call-backs from their potential employers after submitting their CVs. Consider the example in Table 1, where Oksana (35), a Ukrainian migrant woman in Australia, describes her situation to the researcher (Dovchin & Dryden, 2022, p. 379).

Before moving to Australia, Oksana gained her undergraduate and post-graduate degrees in sports science and management from her home country, Ukraine. When she first arrived in Australia, Oksana was very confident about finding a suitable job because of her double degree. Nevertheless, she soon realised that one of the most challenging aspects of being a migrant with a transnational background was finding employment in Australia. As Oksana points out, she ended up unemployed for the first two years and started volunteering at an aged care centre, hoping that she would get a permanent job. She ended up working at a childcare centre, which is entirely different from her university degree. One of the most challenging aspects for Oksana when finding a job was to actually go through the initial screening process, as she explains

Table 1 Interview, May 1 2019, WA (Dovchin & Dryden, 2022, p. 379)

#	Interview (in English)
1.	**Researcher:** Can you tell me more about the challenges you have faced in Australia?
2.	**Oksana:** Yeah. First, I have to change my last name when I was applying for job.
3.	**Researcher:** Job?
4.	**Oksana:** For job, so instead of writing my last name, like last name ends with a suffix-ova
5.	**Oksana:** I was writing my husband's last name because his last name was without a suffix. So, it's like, and my name is Oksana, but just so don't look so much Russian or Ukrainian I was ...
6.	**Oksana:** I was ... I changed my name for Oksana and just and we also in Ukraine have a second name by our father. It's like my father's name is a typical Eastern European male name. So, I'm in passport ...
7.	**Oksana:** ... But here, If I would put this in my CV, everywhere, they would say, where I'm from? Post-Soviet Union country so I didn't put it, so I changed my names and ... Because before that no one was responding to me, I probably sent around like hundreds of CV and I didn't get a response. Until I did some changes.

how she sent her CV to 'hundreds' of employers (line 7) with no apparent success. From Oksana's point of view, her Ukrainian birth name, which embodies the 'post-Soviet Union' essence (line 7), continuously plays against her newly founded life in Australia. Oksana applied for 'hundreds', if not thousands, of jobs, but no single employer out of 'hundreds' responded to her CV (line 7) (see also Dovchin & Dryden, 2022, p. 380). Other research participants who migrated to Australia have also substantiated Oksana's example. As Khulantsetseg (27), a Mongolian migrant to Australia, describes:

> I've probably applied for hundreds and hundreds of jobs in Australia, but I don't think my CV has even been considered because as soon as they open my CV, it has a very odd-looking name. I'm convinced that the employers choose an Australian-sounding name over any Mongolian or foreign-sounding name [when they check the CV]. It is obvious, and it has always been like this, and it is no longer a secret. (Interview, August 11 2019, WA)

Another Mongolian migrant to Australia, Bolor (34), explains, 'maybe they might have rejected me [from job opportunities] assuming, "Hey! We wonder where her name is from! [She] might not even be able to speak English!"' (Dovchin & Dryden, 2022, p. 377).

Some migrants further reveal how their names on their CV may have become a classic definition of 'taste-based discrimination' (Busetta et al., 2018), in which the employer has specific racial or ethnic profiling and preferences that might include translingual name stigma, including personal preferences of other kinds. Employers might discriminate against a migrant background or ethnic applicant irrespective of other information they have about the applicants (Busetta et al., 2018). See Table 2, in which, as a Mongolian-background international student to Australia, Altantulkhuur (36), describes her experiences.

In the extract in Table 2, 'taste-based discrimination' (Busetta et al., 2018) has been applied to Altantulkhuur, who assumes that her birth name on her CV made it clear that she was an ethnic applicant, a non-native English speaker, and a migrant who did not match the desired racial or ethnic profile of the employer. She applied for a retail assistant job at a big fashion store with her Australian and British background housemates with Anglo names such as Justine and Nicole (line 3). While her housemates immediately received a call-back and were recruited, Altantulkhuur was left out because she did not receive any call-back (line 5). This incident made Altantulkhuur suspect that the employer had 'taste-based discrimination': a preference for Australian and British employees over ethnic background employees, including their white skin and blonde hair (line 9). This incident is consistent with the previously described studies,

Table 2 Interview, 9 September 2019, WA

#	Interview transcripts (in Mongolian)	English translation
1.	**Altantulkhuur:** Nereer yalgavarlakh tokhioldoluudtai unekheer olon udaa tulgarch baisan.	The name discrimination is definitely there. I felt it so many times.
2.	**Researcher:** Yaaj?	How?
3.	**Altantulkhuur:** Neg khuvtsasnii delguurt khudaldagchaar orokh geed bi apply khiigeed. Tsug amidarch baisan Australia bas Angli okhiduudtai tsug bugdeeree apply khiigeed. Nemuud ni Justine, Nicole geed 1.	When I applied for fashion store as a retail assistant, some of my housemates also applied. They were all Australian and British. Their names are Justine, Nicole etc.
4.	**Researcher:** Za?	Yeah?
5.	**Altantulkhuur:** Minii ner medeej duudakhad hetsuu baisan baikh. Tegeed nuguu Justine, Nicole geed housemate-uud bugd ter doroo interview-d urigdaad ajild orson.	My name is complicated to pronounce. After a while, all my housemates with names like Justine and Nicole were invited for interviews and almost directly employed.
6.	**Researcher:** Tiim uu?	Really?
7.	**Altantulkhuur:** Tiim. Kharamsaltai ni nad ruu utasdaagui. Bi unekheer khetsuu baisan. Daraa ni Justine nadad native English speaker-uudiig avsan baikhaa gej kheleed. Yagaad gevel khudaldagch nar uilchluulegchteigee yanz burin jijig sajig yummii tukhai yaridag bolokhoor geed.	Yes. Unfortunately, I never heard back anything from that store. I was devastated. Justine told me later that maybe the employers want someone who can speak native English because being a shop assistant means doing a lot of 'small talks' to the customers.
8.	**Researcher:** Hmm. . .	Hmm. . .
9.	**Altantulkhuur:** Nadad bolokhoor ter delguur zugeer tsagaan aristan Angliaar yaridag okhidoo avakhiig iluud uzdeg yum shig sanagdsan. Australiad khuvtsasnii tom delguuruud ruu orvol dandaa tsagaan aristai, shar ustei, aimar Australia accent-tai okhiduud baidag er ni bol.	It sounded to me like they wanted just white girls with proper English for the store's images or something like that. Actually, if you go to fashion stores in Australia, the retail assistants are mostly white, blonde girls with a very heavy Australian accent, which is very common for fashion stores.

which describe ethnic hierarchy as one of the critical indicators of taste-based discrimination as the highest level of discrimination – one between immigrants and local candidates (Busetta et al., 2018). Note also that second-generation immigrants who are born and educated in the host society still face a large amount of taste-based discrimination, with local preferences (Busetta et al., 2018). For someone like Altantulkhuur, a first-generation transnational migrant in Australia, taste-based discrimination may have directly affected her chance of employment due to her ethnic clues, starting from her ethnic name, as the employer relies on signals and other cues from the CV. Transnational migrants' ethnic names, for example, on CVs may be such a clear signal that members of a particular ethnic group are perceived to be less skilled than the local population.

2.3 CV-Whitening

For many transnational migrants, translingual name stigma happens early and is deeply internalised. They feel and see this stigma as soon as they send their CVs to employers, and many of them learn quickly to adopt a coping strategy to 'whiten their CVs' (Kang et al., 2016) – the practice where migrants attempt to avoid anticipated name stigma by minimising or downplaying their ethno-racial clues in job applications by Anglicising their birth names. The CV-whitening practice is, for example, apparent in Oksana's case in Table 1, where she altered her birth name by removing the suffix of her heavily 'post-Soviet sounding/looking' last name (pseudonym) 'Пугачева' ['Pugacheva'], '-ева' ['-eva'], to give it a more Anglo feel (Dovchin & Dryden, 2022, p. 380). Instead, she used her husband's last name, presented with no '-eva' suffix, which may sound more Western or Anglo to locals' ears and eyes (line 5). Whitening her name, therefore, does not necessarily render a disfavoured migrant completely invisible. However, it makes the most damaging features less prominent, as Oksana describes, 'So, it's like, and my name is Oksana, but just so don't look so much Russian or Ukrainian' (line 5) (Interview, 1 May 2019, WA). Oksana's coping strategy, therefore, reminds us of Goffman's (1963) idea of 'covering', where one manages a stigmatised identity through attempting neither to entirely disguise a stigmatised feature nor to downright appear as a member of the majority group. Instead, the goal is to downplay the salience of characteristics that might nurture discrimination. As Goffman (1963, p. 103) notes, 'persons who are ready to admit possession of a stigma (in many cases because it is known about or immediately apparent) may nonetheless make a great effort to keep the stigma from looming large'. After Anglicising her name on her CV,

Oksana finally managed to get a few call-backs, as she mentions in line 7 that no one was responding to her until she used some CV-whitening strategies (Dovchin & Dryden, 2022, pp. 379–81).

The CV-whitening strategy may further apply beyond one's birth name as some transnational migrants seek to whiten other small bits and pieces of translingual orthographic traces that might make their CV look 'foreign', which could potentially hinder them from passing the initial CV screening stage. A migrant from Ukraine, Natasha's CV has been disqualified from the very first stage 'hundreds of times' (Interview, 29 April 2019, WA). She has a PhD degree in educational sciences, a master's degree in psychology, and a bachelor's degree in history from Ukrainian universities. She was a senior lecturer at one of the most prestigious universities in Ukraine, and she published many research articles in English, Russian, and Ukrainian. In fact, Natasha is fluent in those three languages. Natasha was in a privileged and strong academic position in Ukraine, where she was educated and employed by the best academic institutions in the country. All too often, unfortunately, according to Natasha, she found it 'extremely difficult', or at times 'almost impossible', to get secure and fulfilling work in Australia that would match her skills (Interview, 29 April 2019, WA). Natasha's strong image of a genuinely vibrant translingual citizen – a Ukrainian-educated migrant in Australia with the linguistic skills of English, Ukrainian, and Russian – clearly portrayed on her CV, had, in fact, become the rejection basis of how she would likely communicate or perform at work. After living in Australia for almost eleven years, Natasha is still looking for that 'perfect' job after sending out hundreds of CVs (Interview, 29 April 2019, WA). Natasha gets extremely emotional and weeps when she says:

> So many, many experiences, I would always say. When I apply for jobs, I have to change my name. Yeah, it's just really bizarre. Yeah. Yeah. Yeah. And I know many Russian people who have to change their last name. You know, who is looking for a job. They want to change their name because of their CV. They don't want to look like they have some Russian name. (Interview, 29 April 2019, WA)

The strong clues about her professional trajectories, translingual skills, and transnational movements, all taken together, construct a new kind of translingual profile, one that does not, unfortunately, fit the hiring conditions of the employer but one that fits the realities of many struggling transnational identities. So, while Natasha belongs to a truly transnational scale level of mobility, the treatment of her CV is brought down by the employers to an unyielding local institutional order. As a result, Natasha took the advice of other Ukrainian migrants to 'whiten her CV' to pass. Not only did Natasha end up altering her birth name from Ukrainian 'Natasha' to Anglo-sounding 'Natalie', but she also completely removed all the traces of Ukrainian orthographic characteristics in her CV by Anglicising the original names of her alma maters, all in the hope of boosting her chances of getting her desired job. In so doing, Natasha chose to whiten her Ukrainian institutions by Romanising and shortening all the original Ukrainian references. She deliberately Anglicised and shortened her Ukrainian university's original name 'Черкаський національний університет імені Богдана Хмельницького' [The Bohdan Khmelnytsky National University of Cherkasy] simply into 'Cherkasy National University' to make it look more pleasing to the eyes of Australian employers. In so doing, Natasha removed the university's Ukrainian name – Bohdan Khmelnytsky – which was named after the Ukrainian hetman Bohdan Khmelnytsky, born in the Cherkasy region. When she lived in Ukraine, Natasha was extremely proud of her alma mater because it is considered one of the leading universities in Ukraine. In Australia, Natasha is ashamed of her alma mater as its apparent Ukrainian name directly gives away ethnic cues to Australian employers. The same goes for her other alma maters, where she received her academic degrees. For example, her CV shows that the name of the Ukrainian university, 'Уманський державний педагогічний університет імені Павла Тичини' [Pavlo Tychyna Uman State Pedagogical University], was simply Anglicised as 'Uman State Pedagogical University', while the Ukrainian 'Прикарпатський національний університет імені Василя Стефаника' [Vasyl Stefanyk Precarpathian National University]' was shortened and Anglicised as 'Precarpathian National University' (Interview, 29 April 2019, WA). Natasha's CV-whitening strategy seeks to manage the translingual name stigma against her Ukrainianness by diverting the employers' emphasis on her Ukrainianness, which might attract initial stigma. She avoids her CV 'giving off' imaginary stigmas against her linguistic, cultural, and academic background, seeking to distract employers from making quick and superficial judgements about her as an individual.

2.4 Translingual Name Microaggression

Transnational migrants continue to experience disrespect to their names in the host society, and regardless of whether the name of a migrant is intentionally disrespected or someone accidentally butchers the pronunciation, scholars point out that the linguistic, social, and cultural mismatch that causes this interaction is a form of racial microaggression (Lahiri-Roy et al., 2021; Piller, 2016). For example, the quality of service in librarians' written online communications in the UK was examined by Hamer (2021), in which the librarians often addressed non-Anglicised names incorrectly, giving the impression that the librarians were perhaps less familiar with the spelling or structure of the migrants' names. For example, Jinghua, a Chinese student's name, was only correctly addressed by her given name in 16 per cent of responses, compared to over 79 per cent for other Anglo-sounding usernames. As such, the response could seem less welcoming, potentially contributing to discriminating against someone with a non-Anglicised name and a transnational background (Hamer, 2021, p. 8). Incorrectly addressing migrants' names is also common in the classroom context. As Kohli and Solórzano (2012, p. 444) note:

> When a child goes to school, and their name is mispronounced or changed, it can negate the thought, care and significance of the name, and thus the identity of the child. This happens for White and non-White children alike. However, the fact that this experience occurs within a context of historical and continued racism is what makes the negative impact of this experience so powerful for Students of Color.

This section will discuss another common practice of translingual name discrimination, which I call translingual name microaggression – the micro and subtle form of discriminatory practices against migrants' birth name when it is often incorrectly addressed by the mainstream population. This form of microaggression towards migrants' birth names may include mispronunciation, misspelling, misunderstanding, misgendering, mocking, or failing to remember the migrants' birth names, essentially excluding their birth names as not belonging to the naming traditions of the normative majority (Hamer, 2021). The ethnic names may cause inconvenience to the dominant monolingual population because they require them to make an effort or use empathy in actively being involved in learning or appropriately addressing the migrants' names (Hamer, 2021). According to Kohli and Solórzano (2012), the racial microaggression of incorrectly addressing migrants' names is often overlooked due to their subtle implications. Because the insults do not seem to be overt and direct, but rather micro, they may often seem to be regarded as trivial or unimportant (Piller, 2016). However, the cumulative micro-insults against one's name can take their toll on transnational migrants (Kohli & Solórzano, 2012). Consider the example here, where a Mongolian migrant to Australia, whose birth name is Tserenkhand Luvsanjantsan (59), explains:

> When I moved to Australia, no one could pronounce my name correctly. I get tired of correcting my name every time I say my name. My birth name has a deep Buddhist philosophical meaning, which was given by the Buddhist Lama. Since my childhood, it was a big deal for my parents and for me. Since

I came to Australia, my name was not something I was proud of anymore. I officially changed my name from Tserenkhand to Hannah in all my documents to fit in Australia. It really hurt my feelings. Of course, Hannah was easier for everyone because I didn't want to cause any inconvenience to anyone. People are too lazy to pronounce my name correctly. (Interview, 13 October 2018, WA)

Here, Tserenkhand explains that the experience of renaming her birth name hurt her feelings immensely because her name derives from Buddhist tradition in Mongolia, and means 'nobility and dignity'. The name was given by a very popular Buddhist Lama in Mongolia, which is considered a significant honour by many Mongolians. From Tserenkhand's perspective, her name is very personal not only to her, but it also carried a great deal of cultural, traditional, and religious meaning for her family and parents. When she moved to Australia, her birth name lost its cultural, religious, and traditional significance, directly related to Mongolia's long history of Tibetan Buddhist tradition in which naming is considered one of the most honourable practices. Many of Tserenkhand's daily interactants would have been unaware that this form of microaggression would result in Tserenkhand detaching her cultural identity and changing her name and the traditional values around it throughout her life in Australia. It is possible that the discount of her birth name could well be unintentional by many of her interactants. However, if we frame this experience and its negative impact within a larger context of translingual discrimination, it could become a racial microaggression (Takeuchi, 2022). Perceptions regarding the acceptability of one's name are determined intersectionally, along with the speaker's national, ethnic, racial, gender, and socio-economic status (Salonga, 2015), exposing them to multiple levels of bias and discrimination that relate to their other intersectional attributes (Nelson et al., 2016). Tserenkhand mentions an example of translingual name microaggression – a lack of effort or ignorance from the host population in learning the correct pronunciation of migrants' names, which is often outside their linguistic and cultural comfort zone – as she describes that people are 'too lazy' to learn her name correctly (Hamer, 2021). From this perspective, when her identities such as race, ethnicity, nationality, and gender are considered in conjunction with the name discrimination she faces, it paints a much larger picture of how she is excluded and othered. Translingual name discrimination falls within the larger aspect of intersectional identity, where transnational migrants are exposed to multiple levels of discrimination that may also relate to their other intersectional attributes (Nelson et al., 2016).

There have been other examples where our research participants were teased or mocked over their names by peers in the classroom settings. Another

Mongolian woman, Bolortsetseg Amgalanbaatar (34), shares an experience of when she first arrived in Australia as an international student and her tutor made a joke about her name that led to her peers laughing at her. As Bolortsetseg explains:

> In my classroom, I was the only Mongolian, as most international students would be from China or Malaysia and the rest were from Australia. When my tutor did a roll call, it was an embarrassing experience. All Chinese students had English names, and they got away easily. I didn't know I had to change my name to English because it was my first experience in the Australian classroom. When my tutor got to my name, he paused and mispronounced my name. But when I corrected him, he laughed at his mistake, and the whole class started laughing with him. It was an innocent mistake, of course. Everyone was laughing. However, it was so humiliating to me. I was so ashamed that my name caused such an embarrassing situation in the classroom.
>
> (Interview, 19 September 2018, WA)

This incident can be interpreted as a racial microaggression because the tutor's laughing at his own mistake, which encouraged microaggressions from Bolortsetseg's peers in the form of laughter, resulted in a feeling of humiliation for her. While some of her peers were international students like Bolortsetseg, who had possibly experienced name microaggressions like Bolortsetseg as they all had English names, they nevertheless followed the cues of their tutor, contributing to her feeling of humiliation. When the tutor laughed at his own mistake, he probably did not necessarily intend malice or carefully measure the harmful consequences of his actions because, after all, laughter is a simple behaviour (Kohli & Solórzano, 2012). However, the tutor's laughter was a cue to the rest of the students in the class that laughing at someone's name was normal or acceptable. As Lahiri-Roy et al. (2021, p. 11) ask, '[h]ow can we teach about social justice, diversity, and inclusion if we cannot address young people by their name?' When our students are taught 'to tease the unfamiliar, rather than embrace or celebrate an exposure to something new', Lahiri-Roy et al. (2021, p. 11) add, 'it can create a climate of racial hostility for those who are not part of the majority'.

2.5 Renaming Practices

For many migrants, translingual name microaggressions may happen repeatedly, and they profoundly internalise these microaggressions. Many research participants have quickly learned to live a double life to cope with name microaggressions. As a result, they adopt a coping strategy of 'renaming practices' – a common strategy of adopting names that fit English mouths to pronounce and English ears to hear. Such renaming practices have even been found to hold real-life advantages for migrants. Individuals who use an Anglicised name in everyday life may receive notably better overall treatment than those who use their birth names (Lahiri-Roy et al., 2021). Renaming practices can occur in many forms. For example, Romanising one's birth name: that is, transliterating one's birth name into a Roman orthographic system. For example, a Mongolian name, written in Cyrillic Mongolian as 'Болорцэцэг', can be Romanised to English as 'Bolortsetseg'. This strategy, however, seems to be not very useful because when a name does not share a similar phonetic structure across the two languages, it becomes difficult for the receiving end (Thompson, 2006). It is also complicated because names can be lengthy in one culture while in another, for example in Anglo-Saxon culture, names can be short, which may still lead to name microaggressions from the host society. Many research participants described that they initially tried to rename themselves through Romanisation (e.g., from Нинжхорол to Ninjkhorol). While Romanisation may have given some opportunities to their interactants, for example, to be able to read their names, the migrants' name was still frequently incorrectly addressed.

Replacing one's birth name with an Anglo name is a more common form of renaming practice than Romanising for many transnational migrants. Chinese students in Australia, for instance, tend to offer alternative Anglo-sounding names to their lecturers and peers – 'just call me John', or 'you can call me Sarah' – because the majority of people mispronounce their names (Zhang & Noels, 2022). It is embarrassing to hear their names mispronounced, and/or they seek to avoid appearing rude by correcting their teachers or peers when their names are mispronounced (Lahiri-Roy et al., 2021). According to Diao (2014), some Chinese students replace their names with 'English' names during their adolescent years while taking English classes in China, imagining the Anglophone world as being a homogenous society where English names must be used to successfully facilitate communications with native English speakers. Many Chinese students in this study have Anglicised their names from 'Bo' to 'Bob', or 'Fan' to 'Frank' to maintain an approximate sound or orthographic look to their birth names. Alternatively, another major group of Chinese students has entirely replaced their birth names with English – from 'Qian' to 'Lucy', or from 'Ming' to 'Grace'. Overall, renaming practices in an English-speaking environment is a complex process of identity negotiation for many transnational migrants because it is embarrassing to hear their names mispronounced, and they do not want to cause any inconvenience to people around them. For many migrants, 'saving the face value' (Leng, 2005) seems to be expected, as they wish to appear polite and respectful towards their interactants. Ultimately, transnational migrants seek to cope with transnational name microaggressions by adopting their own strategies of renaming their birth names.

2.6 Conclusion

This section discusses one of the primary and most prominent instances of translingual discrimination – translingual name discrimination – where transnational migrants' social, cultural, and economic opportunities are instantly disqualified, and their intrinsic qualities and skills are immediately discounted, often based on their birth name. Because the names and naming practices of transnational migrants may represent their ethnic, cultural, and linguistic identities, they often deviate from the normative naming traditions in the host society. Two of the most common ideologies and practices of translingual name discrimination – translingual name stigma and translingual name microaggressions have been discussed in this section.

Translingual name stigma refers to a collective stigma based on 'imagined' negative attributes associated with transnational migrants purely based on their ethnic-sounding birth names. The birth name may cause stigmas about its carrier being less skilled or less capable than the normative majority, irrespective of their actual backgrounds and skills. Translingual name stigma is primarily found in the initial hiring process of recruitment, when the candidate's CV is examined. This study, for example, found that nearly 80 per cent of the total research participants have revealed that their birth names containing any ethnic or migrant cues leads to fewer call-backs or no response at all. As a result, these transnational migrant-background participants adopt a coping strategy of CV-whitening, in which they seek to downplay their ethno-racial clues to make it easier for host society employers, for example by using alternative English names. Not only do migrants whiten their birth name on a CV, but they also whiten the names and titles of their educational alma maters in the hope of boosting their chances of getting their desired jobs.

Translingual name microaggression is another micro and subtle form of translingual name discrimination practice, in which migrants' birth names are often incorrectly addressed through mispronunciation, misspelling, misunderstanding, misgendering, mocking, or failing to remember the migrants' birth names, essentially excluding their birth names as not belonging to the naming traditions of the normative majority. The cumulative micro-insults against migrants' names can take their toll on the victims as the migrants continue to experience microaggressions towards their birth names. Consequently, they adopt a coping strategy of 'renaming practices', from Romanising their birth names to choosing new English names.

Overall, the data examples show that the first step in maintaining an inclusive multicultural society is to start respecting transnational migrants' birth names. When the mainstream population in the host society, including educators, policymakers, or employers, start practising translingual name discrimination, they convey a colour-blind message to the public that the migrants' racial, ethnic, cultural, and sociolinguistic backgrounds do not matter in the society. While most employers in Australia, for example, seem to explicitly declare their commitment to diversity at face value, they still seem to engage in discrimination against migrants. One's birth name may not seem like a big deal, but these attitudes also show a significant expression of ignorance. Zhang and Noels (2022) note the importance of respecting language minorities' name choices in this regard, calling for social efforts in building an inclusive environment that accepts diverse personal names originating from many different languages.

It is, therefore, essential to raise public awareness that social justice, diversity, and inclusion start from correctly addressing a person's birth name. As Dovchin and Dryden (2022, p. 386) note, 'what would the livelihood of skilled transnational migrants look like if employers interpret their CV tied to an individual's peculiar biographical trajectory?' 'What if employers read their CV as set in a real context and validate their qualifications as a real achievement accomplished by real people?' Language policymakers should consider current linguistic dictums in their policy that prepare national employers for 'foreign-sounding names' as a non-pragmatic issue that is just a surface feature that does not necessarily indicate one's intrinsic values, skills, and competence. The birth names of these transnational migrants should be respected and taken seriously, and should not be tied to any form of authorities' name order or policing.

3 Translingual English Discrimination

3.1 Translingual English Discrimination

The concept of translingual English discrimination in this Element refers to the ideologies and practices that may exclude and discriminate against transnational migrants based on their usage, proficiency, and practices of English (Dovchin & Dryden, 2022). Once these migrants transnationally move from their home countries to new English-dominant host societies, they are likely to become subject to translingual English discrimination as the 'standard' form of English of that host society becomes the one which, within the institutional and interpersonal levels, is the only legitimate and acceptable version (Blommaert, 2010; Milroy & Milroy, 2012). Tupas and Rubdy's (2015, p. 3) conception of 'unequal Englishes' – 'the unequal ways and situations in which Englishes are arranged, configured, and contested' – is important here. English is disproportionately categorised and classified in local contexts across people and institutions with different social, financial, and cultural backgrounds (Pan, 2015). As a result, the position of transnational migrants' English may be transformed into different indicators of English mainly due to their unequal access to standard or 'native' forms of English (Tupas & Rubdy, 2015). Central to the idea of translingual English discrimination is the argument that one's English proficiency includes the ability to converse through appropriate or acceptable forms of Englishes. If it does not, the speakers' social, linguistic, financial, and identity positionings are marginalised (Dovchin et al., 2016). In other words, in examining translingual English discrimination, valuing one's linguistic resources becomes dependent on the identities that possess them rather than the resources themselves (Blommaert, 2010). In this context, English used in English-speaking nations such as the USA, Australia, UK, and Canada may be viewed as authentic and legitimate English. At the same time, any other forms of English are pathologised (J. Lee, 2017).

The racialised ideologies against diverse forms of English in opposition to standard forms of English may define what (il)legitimate English is. At the same time, transnational migrant groups are often framed as 'incapable of producing any legitimate language' (Rosa, 2016, p. 163). As Flores and Rosa (2015, p. 150) note, 'we argue that the ideological construction and value of standardized language practices are anchored in what we term raciolinguistic ideologies that conflate certain racialized bodies with linguistic deficiency unrelated to any objective linguistic practices'. These types of raciolinguistic ideologies construct 'racialized speaking subjects' as 'linguistically deviant' despite their English practices being situated as 'normative or innovative' (Flores & Rosa, 2015, p. 150). This means that particular English practices of transnational migrants can be stigmatised, regardless of whether they correspond to standard English or not (Heller & McElhinny, 2017).

Transnational migrants seem to be considered one of the most vulnerable targets of translingual English discrimination. They can be excluded from all dimensions of social life in the host society because of their translingual English identifications (Tankosić, 2020). They are rarely given the full credit they deserve in terms of their usage of English, and there appear to be considerable unconscious stigmas and stereotypes against their linguistic, cultural, and communicative backgrounds. As De Costa (2020, p. 833) notes, when a speaker is transnationally mobile, 'multilingual and shuttles between different languages and language varieties … more often than not, her ability to translanguage . . . is seen as a liability instead of an asset'. For example, standard English becomes the hiring order of things against which all other diverse forms of English are 'accurately measured' (Ruecker & Ives, 2015). The employers' 'accurate measurement' seems to be the standardised varieties of English, while the linguistic diversity that these transnational migrants bring with them is discounted. As a result, transnational migrants pay 'ethnic penalties' when applying for jobs, based not only on their race and ethnicity but also on their translingual English backgrounds (Li & Campbell, 2009).

Consequently, the extremely proficient English skills of these transnationals, which were highly appreciated in their home countries, may often be deskilled or devalued in the host society, as their translingual English status goes 'from hero to zero', and where highly skilled transnational migrants face 'paradoxes of migrations' (Dovchin & Dryden, 2022, p. 365). That is, highly proficient English users with migrant backgrounds are forced to work in low-skilled areas. For example, a PhD graduate ends up driving a taxi or a straight-A student may fail university assignments (Coates & Carr, 2005; Dovchin & Dryden, 2022). Some of the most common characteristics of translingual English discrimination, which creates the situations of 'ethnic penalties' and 'paradoxes of migrations', are associated with its two main elements – translingual English accentism and translingual English stereotyping. These two elements are simultaneously associated with coping strategies such as 'purification' and 'ethnic evasion'.

3.2 Translingual English Accentism

The element of 'translingual English accentism' refers to the ideologies and practices used to marginalise, contest, and exclude transnational migrants' biographical English accents against any forms of standard-English accents (Dryden & Dovchin, 2021). While migrants' accented English is viewed as audible and problematic and needs to be reduced or eliminated, the standard-English accent is less problematic and unremarkable (Blommaert, 2009; Fang, 2020). Diverse forms of standard-English accents, such as American or British English, become no longer an 'accent' compared to other 'foreign', 'translingual', and 'ethnic' accents (Lippi-Green, 2011; Ramjattan, 2020, 2022). There is unquestioning certainty that British or American is the most desirable and appropriate kind of English, as there are deeply entrenched attitudes and ideologies attached, including an emotional and irrational attachment to British and American English (Jenkins, 2007). According to Munro et al. (2006, p. 71), 'individuals with a foreign accent may be perceived negatively because of the stereotypes or prejudices that accent can evoke in a listener'. Accentism, therefore, may occur when transnational migrants' biographical English accents tend to shape the negative perceptions of their English proficiency, and does not seem to elicit the same treatment as British, Australian,

American, Canadian (and so on) English accents. Accentism is referred to as discrimination against transnational migrants. Following Creese and Kambere (2003, p. 566), 'extra-local', 'foreign', 'ethnic', 'immigrants', and so on 'accents' are constantly disadvantaged by the hegemonic standard-English accents ('Canadian', 'American', 'British', 'Australian', etc.). Standard-English accents, as De Klerk and Bosch (1995, p. 18) note, may often connote 'high status and competence', and native speakers of English are often 'warmly regarded, and people are predisposed to think highly of them'. Transnational migrants' accents, on the other hand, may create disentitlement and a cold reception as they are treated not according to who they are, but according to how they pronounce English, while speaking a non-standard variety of English ultimately transforms migrants into what is only suggested by their accents (Creese & Kambere, 2003).

According to Blommaert (2009), Asian accents such as Indian, Chinese, Korean, Japanese, and Vietnamese tend to be inherently positioned in the danger zone of global English accents, often exposed to linguistic shaming, including labels such as 'peripheral speakers, as incomprehensible or as ridiculous impostors' (Piller, 2016, p. 197). These accents are often mocked in the popular discourse provoked by the bias against migrants with an 'ethnic English accent' (Hanish & Guerra, 2000). Consider the example of our research participant Van (20), a student of Vietnamese background, who migrated to Australia when she was in high school, and who has been suffering from accentism due to her 'Vietnamese accented English'. Van feels vulnerable and self-conscious when she speaks English with local Australians. When she first arrived in Australia from Vietnam and started attending a local high school, her classmates started laughing at her English accent: 'at school, people laughed at me. . . . they were laughing because I was pronouncing wrongly' (Interview, 9 October 2018, WA). The 'Vietnamese accented English' spoken by Van became a laughing matter for her classmates, which further developed into chronic bullying. As Van further describes, 'it was like I was in the class sitting in the group, and then I accidentally talked like . . . hmmm . . . pronounced wrongly. One or two. And then they burst into a laugh, and then I feel like maybe I should shut my mouth and say nothing at all. . . . It was a constant bully' (Interview, 9 October 2018, WA; cf. Dovchin, 2020b). Van's encounter with accentism occurred in the form of 'laughter' – an overt form of accentism, consisting of 'practices when people explicitly mock, imitate, or make jokes about one's English accents and these practices may often include the pre-defined ideologies such as stigmas and stereotypes about the race, ethnicity, or culture which they are mocking' (Dryden & Dovchin, 2021, pp. 3–4). This type of overt accentism, especially in the form of laughing, is a frequent occurrence for many transnational migrants. An international student from Mongolia, Chimeg (40), describes 'people [Australians] would laugh at me when I pronounce certain words. Maybe, they didn't mean it bad, but it still hurts' (Dovchin, 2020b, p. 810).

Another form of laughing at or teasing over one's accent has been apparent in the context of our research participants, especially female participants with Eastern European English accents. For example, Nadya (35) from Ukraine has experienced overt accentism in the workplace when she worked as a coordinator at a childcare centre. Nadya recalls the incidents where her Ukrainian-accented English was mocked by her Australian female co-workers. As Nadya recalls:

> I worked with younger girls. So, when I went there and as a coordinator, sometimes I have to point on the stuff that is . . . it's not done proper. I have to say this and that and reaction would they have one time. I turned around and I saw they were making faces about my accent just like [facial demonstration]. I just turned around because, like, at work I got used to look everywhere because of the children stuff. I have to like multitask, and while I was talking, I turned around, and they behind me were just like making fun of the accent. They were just saying, like, all like [facial demonstration] like [facial demonstration]. That funny face, then. And, and, also like they were actually like copying my words and the way how I say. (Tankosić & Dovchin, 2021, p. 15)

Here, Nadya recalls how she lost her authority as a coordinator to her young Australian assistants when her Ukrainian English accent became a point of overt mockery through 'making faces'. Nadya recalls how these assistants were pantomiming the way she speaks through facial demonstrations, while also copying and mimicking certain words Nadya pronounces. Nadya feels she lost professional credibility because her accent overpowered her 'senior' position in the workplace, and she felt less powerful and less capable than her assistants (Tankosić & Dovchin, 2021).

This type of overt accentism against Eastern European English accents is also reminiscent of the public evaluation of the 'accent' of Melania Trump, wife of former President of the USA Donald Trump, and a native of Slovenia, who does not speak English as her first language. For many social media users, as J. Lee (2017, p. 48) notes, her 'accent' was pathologised through sexist rhetoric such as a 'sexy or hot accent' but also the xenophobic rhetoric of sounding like a 'hooker', 'bitch', and 'prostitute'. In a similar vein to Melania Trump, Bolor, a Mongolian female student in Australia, started experiencing accentism when she moved to Australia based on how she speaks English, or to be more specific, a Russian-accented Mongolian-English (Dovchin, 2019b, pp. 90–3). Mongolians commonly use Russian-accented English due to Mongolia's early sociolinguistic background. Mongolia was a satellite of the former Soviet Union for nearly seventy years, from 1921 to 1990. Under this Soviet rule, Russian linguistic and cultural elements were most prominent for political discourse and social mobility. From the 1960s, the Russian language was taught as a compulsory foreign language for general public schools, while many Mongolians started studying in the Soviet Union at a tertiary level. During this time, the Mongolian language started absorbing many loan words from the Russian language, which are still commonly used in Mongolia (Marzluf & Saruul-Erdene, 2019). Overall, the Russian language as a main foreign language was already deeply absorbed into the sociolinguistic background of Mongolians when English started taking a larger role and replacing the once-popular Russian language in 1990, when Mongolia transformed itself from a socialist to a democratic society. Mongolians started learning English from Russian textbooks, and many Russian language teachers took the responsibility of teaching English instead of Russian. As a result, Mongolians in the post-socialist context who started learning English acquired a heavily Russian-accented English. From this perspective, Bolor's use of English illustrates some classic examples of a translingual English accent, in which the standard phonetic form of English is heavily Russian-accented, as if she is speaking English through Russian (Dovchin, 2019b). She pronounces the English phrase 'Hi, where were you?' as 'Hi, vair ver you?', and, when using the fricative consonant /h/ in words such as 'how' and 'happy', may seem to sound them in the mouth /x/ rather than in the throat /h/. Further, English dental fricatives /θ/ and /ð/ are also often replaced with /s/ and /z/ by Bolor, as she pronounces expressions such as 'mother' [/'mʌðəʳ/] as '/'mʌzəʳ/' or 'thunder' ['/'θʌndə(r)/'] as '/-'sʌndə(r)/'. Bolor also incorporates a large amount of Russian and Mongolian linguistically mixed expressions and terms when she speaks English (Dovchin, 2019b, p. 91). Some examples are: 'mashin tereg' ['a car or something like that'] – the combination of the Russian root term, 'машина' ['car'] with the Mongolian phrase 'tereg' ['cart'], and 'diploom' bolokhguishd' ['diploma didn't work'], through lengthening the sound 'o' in the original Russian word, 'диплом' ['diploma'] into the Mongolian phonetic system 'diploom', while also adding the Mongolian phrase 'bolokhguishd' ['didn't work'].

Because of her strong Russian-accented Mongolian-English, Bolor experienced translingual accentism, as some 'guys' and 'men' in Australia started teasing or making jokes about how her English sounds 'sexy'. As Bolor describes:

> I didn't know how to take it when men said that my English sounded 'sexy'. As a compliment or disgrace? I was confused. I didn't know how to respond, but I was not feeling good about it. I couldn't figure out why I was speaking

'sexy' English and started becoming quite self-conscious when I started speaking English with my males, for example. I definitely didn't want to feel sexualized the way how I spoke English. (Dovchin, 2019b, p. 92)

Initially, Bolor could not understand why her accent was viewed as 'sexy' by some men in Australia. She found it intimidating when the opposite sex openly acknowledged their affection for her accent. As a young student from Mongolia, she did not fully comprehend the stigmas about Russian-accented English in the West. Similarly, the participant Nadya's Ukrainian-accented English was sexualised by some Australians, particularly men, who not only commented that her accent was 'sexy' but also asked whether she was a 'Russian bride' in the past (Dryden & Dovchin, 2021, p. 8). This is just one example of the belittling linguistic and cultural stereotyping surrounding Eastern European women, which posits that they immorally use their sexuality for financial and citizenship reasons (Tankosić, 2020). As we have noted in our study, 'the sexualization of Nadya's accent is a label that is placed on her because she speaks with a foreign accent and reduces her identity to a sexualized and stereotyped caricature of what Eastern European women are perceived to be, according to their accent, nationality, socio-economic status and gender' (Dryden & Dovchin, 2021, p. 8). This is also a reminder that certain transnational groups are particularly stigmatised, such as Eastern European or East Asian women being stereotyped as marrying for economic and visa purposes, so-called 'mail order brides' (Tankosić, 2020), or as perpetual foreigners who will never fully belong in the host society (Lee et al., 2009).

Accentism can further create the situation of 'ethnic penalties' in the labour market, in which translingual migrants may become the victims of 'paradoxes of migration', where their professional, educational, and linguistic skills can transform from 'hero to zero' despite their skilled work visas and permanent residency being granted based on their highly valuable professional skills (Dovchin & Dryden, 2022, p. 365). As Dovchin and Dryden (2022, p. 372) note, 'while many migrants are granted permanent residence and are invited to migrate to the host society primarily based on their past valuable professional skills, the employers in the host society, in fact, place little or no value on their skills after their arrival'. When, for example, Khulan (27) lived in Mongolia, her country of origin, she was often 'hailed as a hero' because of her high level of English skills and education. However, since she migrated to Australia, her Mongolian-accented English put her into a 'zero' position. According to Khulan, her English was never corrected or questioned in Mongolia (Dovchin & Dryden, 2022, p. 372). However, her English, especially her English accent, has become a 'laughing stock' in Australia and her accent has been corrected multiple times by locals (Interview, 5 August 2019, WA). Khulan remembers one incident which deeply hurt her because it happened in a formal situation, where she was desperately trying to please her interactants. During a job interview, Khulan mispronounced 'Very' as 'Worry', and she started getting extremely anxious: 'I think I mispronounced "Very" as "Worry" ... Then, a woman [in the selection committee] loudly corrected it as "Very Very"!' While the woman on the selection committee corrected Khulan's mispronunciation in a loud and authoritative way of 'Very! Very!' she also added another layer of overt accentism by mocking her accent as 'truly international' (Interview, 5 August 2019, WA). As Khulan describes, 'they laughed sarcastically, saying that my accent was kind of "truly international"!' (Dovchin & Dryden, 2022, p. 382). In this context, Khulan's translingual English accent does not systematically fit the hiring condition of the employers in the selection committee, but does fit the sad reality that transnational migrants encounter daily. The Mongolian-accented English Khulan had brought with her from Mongolia negated all her credentials during her transnational movement, as she was penalised for mispronouncing English (Dovchin & Dryden, 2022, p. 382).

Accentism can also happen in a covert and subtle form when English users with transnational backgrounds are silently excluded from social life and other opportunities because of their accented English (Dryden & Dovchin, 2021). The offenders may not fully be aware of their discriminative actions because they are already blinded by broader structural standard-English accent ideologies. A type of covert accentism can be practised through indirect subordination of minorities or disadvantaged groups, for example by 'social exclusion' – the act of rejecting someone from interpersonal interactions, including peer interaction or participation in a community (Tankosić & Dovchin, 2021). Social exclusion may look harmless on the surface; however, in the essence of basic human interaction, social exclusion can be analogous to being subject to the lowest levels of social hierarchy. Even though covert accentism does not have to be direct, physical, or verbal, and is sometimes not even intentional, it seems familiar across our research participants (see Table 3).

In Table 3, our research participant, Narangerel (42), a Mongolian-background full-time mum living in Australia, shares her multiple encounters of feeling excluded from social gatherings like mums' groups from her son's school (line 1). Narangerel believes this behaviour points to a lack of communication interest or even empathy from local mums, which leads Narangerel to assume that the Australian mums in her group do not wish to make an effort to get to know her as a migrant mum, do not recognise her experience as a migrant mum in Australia, or take their time to listen to and process Narangerel's accent (line 5). Narangerel demonstrates that she tries to accommodate other mums in her repertoire by repeating herself to make sure everyone in the group

Table 3 Interview, 7 September 2018, WA

#	Interview transcript (in Mongolian)	English translation
1.	**Narangerel:** Jishee ni, khuugiinkhee mom's groupt khaaya ochikhoor namaig erduusuu yariandaa oruuldaggui shuudee. Australia mom nar.	For example, I don't feel I'm included in the conversation fully when I'm in the mom's group with Australian moms.
2.	**Researcher:** Yagaad?	Why not?
3.	**Narangerel:** Minii accentiig sain oilgoddoggui baikh gej boddog shuu. Minii English-iig sain oilgoddoggui baikh aa! Tegeed l bi eerch muuraad dakhij davtaad l khelsen yumaa dakhiaad l khelne. Ted nariig oilgotol ni.	Because I think they don't understand my accent and it is maybe hard for them to understand my English! So, I always repeat and stutter what I've said to make sure they understand.
4.	**Researcher:** Aan tiim gejuu?	You think so?
5.	**Narangerel:** Tiimee! Tegeed namaig yariandaa oruulakhaasaa tuvugshuuguud tsuglarakhaaraa. Unekheer gutamshigtai! Namaig yariaad l ekhlekheer nad ruu neg kharaad l ungurnu. Tegeed minii khelj baigaa yumiig ogt tookhgui. Yamar ch comment baikhgui. Yu ch baikhgui! Bi zugeer l neg tsagaach. Minii duu khooloi yamar chi une tsenegui.	Yes! So, they kind of avoid talking to me when we gather. It is very humiliating! When I talk, they look at me, but they just ignore what I say. No comments. Nothing! I'm just a migrant. Nobody cares about my voice.

understands her, which sometimes leads to 'stuttering' (line 3). Nevertheless, her effort is not often reciprocated by other mums by responding or including her in the conversation, as they decide that her accent is incomprehensible (line 3; line 5). Hence, her participation in the conversation requires Narangerel to work harder in her communication because other mums are not inclusive, sympathetic, or accustomed to her accent.

From these perspectives, all these migrants experience reluctance from the mainstream population to sympathise with their accented English, and this lack of sympathy further creates situations where they are silently excluded from full participation in social life. Hence, peer interactions prevent Narangerel from integrating into the local community, causing social disconnection and division, and a lack of local friendships (Khvorostianov & Remennick, 2017). This example also demonstrates that covert accentism is perpetuated by a power imbalance, as it puts the disadvantaged group behind the privileged local society, leading to unfavourable behaviour directed at its supposedly inferior members (Fox & Stallworth, 2005). Upon hearing migrants' accented English, the mainstream population seems to make 'a conscious or sub-conscious decision whether they will participate or not' (Dryden & Dovchin, 2021, p. 10). They may further 'reject that participation' if the migrants' accents are deemed 'incomprehensible' (Dryden & Dovchin, 2021, p. 10), creating a silent social exclusion. Such social exclusion, based on one's accent, is veiled, subtle, and hidden, but harmful to transnational migrants.

Overall, accentism may lead to the development of adverse psychological and emotional effects. As seen in our examples, migrants may start questioning their own intelligibility and competence, or even think their excluded accent means they are stupid. In some cases, people with an accented English from a particular race and ethnicity can be stigmatised as less sophisticated or lacking intelligence, and may often be seen as intellectually slower when compared to native English users (Clément & Gardner, 2001). They may be viewed as having communication and language problems that make them 'unsuitable' for any type of social communication (Rosa, 2016). Our research participants largely describe the discourse of intelligence deficiencies in terms of accentism: Sofia from Ukraine described her feeling of 'being less cool' – 'I felt like I was so uncool and unpopular among locals sometimes. Like a second [class] citizen'; Yulia noted her feeling of being 'stupid' 'because you can't represent yourself because of language, people can think that you're stupid, you're silly, you don't deserve good treatment'; Natasha reported her mistreatment by being viewed as 'stupid' and 'uneducated' – 'sometimes people treat you, if you are not good at language, they, I feel they treat you like you let's say, stupid, not educated enough' (Tankosić & Dovchin, 2021, p. 16). Likewise, Narangerel from Mongolia felt humiliated and stupid: 'I started doubting my own self when people started questioning my English. I felt so stupid' (Interview, 7 September 2018, WA); Wang from China describes, 'I started feeling really really stupid once I arrived in Australia because people didn't understand what I said' (Interview, 23 April 2019, WA).

3.3 Translingual English Stereotyping and Hallucination

Another popular element of translingual English discrimination is translingual English stereotyping. Here, English users with transnational migrant backgrounds are often stereotyped as having low proficiency in English regardless of their actual fluent English skills (Dovchin, 2020b; Piller, 2016). Transnational migrants' usage and practices of English are never judged in separation from their race, ethnicity, look, and physical appearance, as the status of their English can be superficially judged based on literally how they look. According to Lippi-Green (2011, p. 285), 'Native English speakers are willing to judge Asian learners of English – their intelligence, friendliness, work ethic and many other complex personality traits – on the basis of very little information – as long as there is no ambiguity about race. That is, race sometimes has more of an effect than actual English language skills when such judgments are made.' Translingual English stereotyping therefore intersects with the processes of racialisation as migrants may face linguistic problems in their daily lives because their race silently labels them as 'Indian', 'Black', 'Chinese', etc. They are discriminated against not because they have difficulty with communication or comprehension with English (Creese & Kambere, 2003, p. 568), but because 'stereotyping from that particular race' (Clément & Gardner, 2001) is, unfortunately, common towards transnational migrants. Translingual English stereotyping may, therefore, have 'a profound influence on our subconscious attitudes to languages and to speakers of these languages', representing 'the dark side of the human abstraction process' (De Klerk & Bosch, 1995, p. 18). This element reminds us of a now-classic experiment conducted in the 1980s at a university in Florida. A native speaker of American English with a standard American-English accent audio-recorded a lecture, which was later played to two different groups of undergraduate students (Piller, 2016, p. 53). The audio-recording was showcased by the image of a Caucasian woman in one case and the image of an Asian woman in the other. A 'foreign', 'non-native', and 'Asian' accent, followed by reduced comprehension and low-level quality of learning experience, was reported by the students who viewed the Asian lecturer despite the absence of that auditory signal (Piller, 2016, p. 53). In a slightly different context, some African-background female migrants in Canada report cases of systemic linguistic discrimination as their African background and African appearance automatically mark them out as an 'African English speaker' or 'Black English speaker' – the equivalent of 'second-rate', 'vernacular', or low level of English. As Creese and Kambere (2003, p. 570) note, 'African women are marked as "Other" through the intonations of their voices and the colour of their skin; indeed, the former implies the latter.' The silent question of 'What colour is your English?' is common (Creese & Kambere, 2003, p. 567).

For example, Ilhan (21), a Somali Muslim woman, grew up in New Zealand. Her parents migrated to New Zealand from Somalia when she was only three years old. She went to school in New Zealand and grew up speaking English as a first language. In fact, her English proficiency is evidently stronger than her heritage language, Somali. However, Ilhan has experienced translingual English stereotyping, mainly due to how she looks, throughout her life in both New Zealand and Australia. Ilhan is a proud Somali Muslim woman who wears a hijab (a head covering worn in public by some Muslim women) and abaya (a traditional robe-like dress worn by some women in parts of the Muslim world, including in North Africa and the Arabian Peninsula). Due to her ethnicity, race, and skin colour, complemented by her ethnic garments like her hijab and abaya, Ilhan indicates that many White people are genuinely shocked by her fluent English as soon as she opens her mouth: 'So when people [White Australians] first hear me, they have this shock on their faces.' Then these people respond to her English fluency through passing comments such as 'Oh, my gosh! Your English is so good! Where did you learn it?' without realising the fact that Ilhan's first language is English (Interview, 28 November 2018, WA). Because she wears a hijab and abaya, translingual English stereotyping becomes obvious as people immediately stereotype her as an ethnic Muslim who possibly is unable to speak English, regardless of her fluency in English as a first-language speaker (see also Dovchin, 2020b, pp. 813–15).

There are also some examples where our research participants have experienced translingual English hallucination, in which transnational migrants' English accent is grossly exaggerated and imagined in the minds of some native speakers of English as they start hearing a foreign accent that is non-existent (Fought, 2006; Lippi-Green, 2011). In her studies on accent discrimination in education, Fought (2006), for example, illustrates the evidence that the human mind is capable of manufacturing or imagining accents where none exist, a phenomenon she calls 'accent hallucination'. She concludes that it is 'possible for expectations about language and ethnicity to override the actual linguistic nature of an individual speech in the minds of hearers' (Fought, 2006, p. 188). In this regard, according to Lippi-Green (2011, p. 285), first-language-English speakers are not necessarily good at identifying Asian accents based on 'voice alone', yet many people believe that they are actually 'quite capable of distinguishing', for example, 'Japanese from Chinese, or India from Pakistan'. Nevertheless, in a situation or context where the speakers actually see each other, 'the non-Asian will sometimes hear a foreign accent that is not there' (Lippi-Green, 2011, p. 285). This phenomenon of accent hallucination commonly occurs across the Asian background transnational migrants in our study. Consider the example in Table 4, in which an Australian-born Indian participant, Chopra (21), describes his multiple experiences with accent hallucination.

In Table 4, Chopra describes his experience with translingual English hallucination, as his fluent Australian English accent is often imagined in the minds

Table 4 Interview, 25 April 2019, WA

#	Interview transcript (in English)
1	**Chopra:** When people see me as an Indian. My brown skin colour. They believe that my English has an Indian accent.
2.	**Researcher:** How often do you feel that?
3.	**Chopra:** Too many times. It is countless. I was born in Australia. I lived in Australia all my life, but as soon as people see my brown skin, they believe my English is Indian.
4.	**Researcher:** OK.

of his interlocutors as 'Indian'. Chopra was born in Australia to Indian parents and his English has a strong Australian standard-English accent (line 1). Nevertheless, Chopra has encountered translingual English hallucination so often (line 3) that it is almost like a norm, because the native speakers of English, because of his skin colour and his Indian appearance (line 1), hear an Indian accent that is non-existent in his linguistic repertoire. In other words, Chopra's interlocutors are capable of manufacturing or imagining a non-existent Indian accent in Chopra's speech as Chopra's ethnicity and race often override the actual linguistic nature of his speech (Fought, 2006).

In a similar vein to Chopra, Wang, who is from a Chinese background, shares his multiple experiences with hallucination: 'even if your English is all right . . .. Even if you speak English really, really good, people still think you have an accent or something. Because you look Asian. People still automatically think because you are automatically connected with very Asian traits' (Interview, 23 April 2019, WA). Wang started learning English at a very young age in China. He went to a primary school where English was the medium of instruction until he moved to Canada to continue his studies at a Canadian high school. As a result, he speaks fluent English with a very strong North American accent. Despite his full proficiency in North American English, Wang's English is deeply shaped by his race and ethnicity, including his Chinese traits, as his 'Chinese face' gives people the false idea that his English has the sound of 'Chinese English' (Dovchin, 2020b).

3.4 Translingual English Purification and Ethnic Evasion

According to Piller (2016, p. 203), learning and using English means 'to become alive to one's marginality in English and a perpetual falling short of the imagined ideal of "perfect" homogeneous English'. For many transnational migrants, 'the purification of one's translingual English accent' – the effort of reducing one's biographical English accent and pronunciation in order to replace it with a proper or standard-English accent – seems to be a common practice (Blommaert, 2009; Dovchin, 2020b). Since the existing biographical accents are wrong and unaccepted, transnational migrants adopt a coping strategy by investing a lot of time and effort into 'purifying' their accented English (Dovchin, 2020b). As Blommaert (2009, p. 253) reminds us, 'at the core of this process of purification [of accent], we see an image of the regimented, subject, someone who can face the challenges of postmodern, globalized existence provided he/she submits to the process of purification and, consequently, sacrifices his/her individual agency in a quest for uniformity and homogeneity'. For example, Zhang (19), a Chinese university student in Australia, describes her daily efforts to purify her Chinese accented English: 'I watch tons of YouTube videos, observing how local Australians talk to each other' (Interview, 11 November 2018, WA); Van, a Vietnamese background student in Australia, explains that her purification of a Vietnamese accented English is the outcome of hard work and rigorous practise – for example watching Australian news, listening to Australian music, and hearing conversations between locals (Dovchin, 2020b, pp. 809–11). Dorj (21), a Mongolian university student in Australia, describes that he watches and listens to Australian news almost every day and copies the presenters' pronunciations: 'I mimic their accents over and over' (Interview, 1 December 2018, WA). Unfortunately, he did not find it helpful, and he started taking online courses to learn an Australian accent. Such courses are offered by online business providers to specific migrant groups of customers like Dorj, who are in search of success in the Australian labour market. Dorj's example reminds us of Blommaert's (2009, p. 243) study on online courses of American accents, which stress uniformity and homogeneity, producing an American accent that replaces existing 'foreign' (i.e., authentic, biographical) accents. The procedures used by such online providers are 'instances of language policing aimed at the infinitely small stuff of language – pronunciation' (Blommaert, 2009, p. 243). They produce language norms within a globalised environment while promoting the ideology that the American accent may bring 'personal happiness, more self-confidence, smooth and efficient communication with Americans, job satisfaction, business opportunities and money' (Blommaert, 2009, p. 252).

During the accent purification process, some migrants go to extreme lengths where they use the coping strategy of 'ethnic ambivalence' or 'ethnic evasion' (Tse, 1998, p. 21), as they start developing little interest or no interest at all in their heritage language. According to Dovchin (2019a, p. 339), 'Speakers with immigrant backgrounds may go through a strong phase where they start rejecting their heritage culture and language because their desire to integrate into the target language and culture is so strong.' Note the example in Table 5, where Natasha (51), a Ukrainian migrant in Australia, still maintains a strong desire to purify her accent and adapt it to the 'Australian way' to avoid any potential social exclusion.

In Table 5, Natasha describes her effort not only to purify her accent and more broadly her English (line 10), but also her ethnic evasion strategy to avoid her own Ukrainian community (line 8) by socialising with only Australians (line 8). Natasha also challenges the popular discourse in Australia that migrants are not willing to integrate into the mainstream culture because, according to Natasha, she definitely makes an effort learn the Australian way of living and its culture (line 8). For Natasha, it is not just about acquiring standard Australian English and its component of an Australian English accent, but even more about avoiding her own ethnic community groups in order to properly integrate into the Australian culture and language (lines 8, 10). This example illustrates a common trend also practised among some Mongolian-background women in Australia, who desperately seek to linguistically pass as 'an insider Australian': that is, to speak like an Australian, to act like an Australian, and even to 'eat like an

Table 5 Interview, 1 May 2019, WA

#	Interview transcript (in English)
1.	**Researcher:** So, you don't really have many Australian friends?
2.	**Natasha:** Umm, no. I would say . . .
3.	**Researcher:** And you lived here for ten years?
4.	**Natasha:** Yes.
5.	**Researcher:** And you think you made an effort to make friends, right?
6.	**Natasha:** Yes, I did. I made effort.
7.	**Researcher:** Because usually they say that immigrants, they don't make efforts. They just want to hang out with themselves.
8.	**Natasha:** No, that is not true, because at one point when I arrived in Australia, I actually didn't want to be so much in my own country community. Like, Ukrainians, they have community, Russians, they have community. I felt like if I'm in Australia, I have to be more involved in this [local] community. So, I have to learn their culture and everything, so I haven't communicated with any post-Soviet Union's people probably like around two years.
9.	**Researcher:** Yeah.
10.	**Natasha:** I was like that. Because I have to learn English and everything. I found after that, I . . . I actually didn't have any people around me. So, I don't actually have a choice.

Australian' (Dovchin, 2019a). Because migrants constantly struggle with accent issues, they have become excessively self-conscious when they speak to White people. They obsess over their pronunciation and how they sound, experiencing fear and anxiety that their merit will be measured by the way they speak English, not what they say.

Cho et al. (2004) caution us that 'ethnic ambivalence' is real. Because they feel humiliated and ashamed of using their heritage languages, they avoid using them (Dovchin, 2019a). These language users would purposely speak only English to their parents if there was a visitor, even though their household language was not English (Orellana et al., 1999). Orellana et al. (1999), for example, present the case where a Mexican immigrant in the USA avoids speaking Spanish because people would think he is from Mexico. A probable contributor to ethnic ambivalence is often caused by 'source of shame', 'correction', and 'ridicule' from dominant speakers. It is observed that ethnic ambivalence can be real in the context of Mongolian-background children living in Australia. Many Mongolian parents living in Australia have pointed out that they have evaded their heritage language – Mongolian – for their children. They have no desire or interest in teaching Mongolian to their children because they do not see any intrinsic value in it. A mother of two, Saruul (35), explains, 'I do not see any value of using Mongolian in Australia. So, I do not speak Mongolian to my kids. I do not teach them Mongolian. They are better off improving their English, and I don't want to confuse their brain' (Interview, 7 September 2019, WA). Similarly, Bolor, also from Mongolia, also gives us a glimpse into why she refuses to speak Mongolian because she started feeling that it was not necessary to use her heritage language, choosing only to speak English. As Bolor explains:

> After living in Australia for a few years, you know the people. You know what to expect. You are quite familiar with the society. You have experienced discrimination, racism, injustice, and bully. Then you have this tendency to stop seeing many Mongolians. You kind of realize that there is really no point in hanging out with Mongolians because you want to integrate into society. You realize that my native language is really useless. In fact, it's a source of shame. When I speak Mongolian, people start judging me. I stop seeing many Mongolians or other immigrants. I would have finished my university and I don't hang out with international students anymore. (Interview, 1 August 2018, WA) (See also, Dovchin, 2019a, p. 346.)

These examples are also reflected among Italian and Greek migrants in Australia, who are losing their language faster than any other migrant groups in Australia. Despite their large populations in Australia, there has been a major decline in people speaking Italian and Greek at home. This may have occurred because most post-war Italian migrants in Australia spoke only specific dialects as their first language, and in the context of the white Australia policy and the imperative to assimilate, they did not pass on their dialects to the second generation. This resulted in the grim situation of grandchildren being unable to talk to their grandparents. The same tragic situation is looming over the second generation of Mongolian children in Australia. Many Mongolians settling in Australia do not use the Mongolian language in their households. Even when both parents are Mongolian, they seem to be encouraging their children to speak 'English only' both at school and home because their goal, understandably, like that of the Italians and Greeks, is to assimilate their children into their new community. The parents have misconceptions about being bilingual and, like many in Australia, have a monolingual mindset and, with English as the dominant language, they believe that by using English as much as possible, their children might have the best chance of prospering in mainstream society. As a result, the importance of passing one's mother language to the next generation is often overlooked (Dovchin, 2019a).

3.5 Conclusion

In this section, the notion of translingual English discrimination refers to the ideologies and practices that may exclude and discriminate against transnational migrants based on their usage, proficiency, and practices of English. When transnational migrants move from their home countries to new English-speaking host societies, their English becomes subject to discrimination as the form of standard English of that host society is the only legitimate or accepted English. Translingual English discrimination is highlighted through its two main elements: accentism and stereotyping and hallucination.

Translingual English accentism refers to the ideologies and practices used to marginalise, contest, and exclude transnational migrants' biographical English accents against any other type of standard-English accents. While migrants' foreign- or ethnic-accented English is viewed as problematic and hence needs to be eliminated, standard-English accents such as British, Australian, American, Canadian English accents are considered unproblematic and normal. Accentism may occur in both overt and covert forms when transnational migrants' biographical English accents may cause negative perceptions of their actual English proficiency. An overt form of accentism may occur in explicit mockery, jokes, or laughter from the interlocutors, but also in the form of direct intimidation, sexualisation, or even as penalisation in job interviews. Accentism can also happen in a covert and subtle form when English users with a transnational migrant background are silently excluded from social life and other social opportunities. A covert form of accentism may, for example, occur in the form of social exclusion – the act of rejecting someone with accented English from peer interactions. Some of our research participants' communication is not often reciprocated by their interlocutors in the conversation. It requires migrants to work harder in their communication because their interlocutors are not inclusive or sympathetic towards their accents. The subtle form of accentism may look harmless on the surface. However, in the essence of basic human interaction, social exclusion could be analogous to being subject to the lowest levels of social hierarchy.

The notion of translingual English stereotyping refers to the pre-defined negative judgements against transnational migrants' English proficiency, where they are not expected to speak English well or may not be heard to speak English well, irrespective of their actual English proficiency. When these migrants are using pre-labelled Englishes, such as 'English spoken by Mongolians' or 'English spoken by Ukrainians', combined with their ethnic, racial, and cultural backgrounds, physical appearance, and look, they are often heard, seen, or imagined to speak 'bad' or 'low proficiency' English irrespective of their actual, highly proficient level in English. Translingual English stereo-typing also creates accent hallucination, in which transnational migrants' English accents are grossly imagined and exaggerated in the minds of some native speakers of English as they hear a foreign accent that is non-existent.

Because of the accumulation of these constant negative experiences of translingual English discrimination elements, many transnational migrants adopt coping strategies such as 'purifying their biographical accent' through daily accent reduction and elimination exercises. They rigorously drill their accents to reduce their biographical accent, from watching local news and videos to going to extreme lengths where they take online accent purification courses. During the purification of accent process, some transnational migrants adopt a strategy of 'ethnic evasion', as they may have no interest in their heritage language and culture, and purposely speak only English. At the same time, they evade socialising with their ethnic group and using their heritage languages.

Overall, this section is timely, considering the sociolinguistic implications of English in current Australian society. There is still a distinct lack of public understanding and a significant gap in public knowledge on transnational migrants' potential for, or early signs of, low social integration, and on chal-lenges of linguistic, cultural, racial, or religious intolerance. It is vital to raise public awareness that translingual English discrimination against migrants may directly be linked to the type of English they use. The section suggests that translingual English discrimination in the areas of accentism, stereotyping, and hallucination must be taken seriously by the mainstream population, policy-makers, educators, and employers.

Raising awareness of the subtle power of translingual English discrimination, such as the types discussed in this section, is therefore essential to achieve a culturally conscious, critical, and inclusive form of bi/multilingual society which promotes co-existence, harmony, and prosperity among multilingual communities (Dovchin, 2020a, 2020b). Translingual English discrimination urges us as language scholars – that is, as public intellectuals and intellectual activists – to pragmatically apply our research into real life by becoming our informants' voices and revealing their lived experiences and realities to address broader issues of racism, social injustice, language activism, and other human rights issues. As Dryden and Dovchin (2021, p. 11) note, 'Part of this may also involve the encouragement of the mindset that understanding communicative exchanges is an act done by both interlocutors attempting to accommodate each other.' However, the realisation of change will largely depend on developing a public consciousness in the mainstream population regarding translingual English discrimination and its adverse effects (Ramjattan, 2022; Takeuchi, 2022).

4 Translingual Discrimination and Emotionality

4.1 Translingual Discrimination and Emotionality

Transnational migrants who become the victims of translingual discrimin-ation are often deprived of living a meaningful social life. The accumulation of chains of discriminative events about their language practices such as translingual name discrimination (section 2), accentism (section 3), and stereotyping (section 3), and their coping strategies and efforts to combat translingual discrimination, including CV-whitening (section 2), renaming one's birth name (section 2), accent purification (section 3), and ethnic evasion (section 3), can have negative impacts on migrants' emotionality, which may lead to serious physical and mental consequences (Dovchin, 2020b, 2021). The struggles of translingual migrants who are using English as an additional language are real, as Rishel and Miller (2017, p. 7) caution us that the systemic exclusion of what translingual English learners and users bring, for example to educational experience, leads them to live a life that parallels other groups who are at risk of contemplating suicide or engaging in other risky self-harming behaviours. Zhang and Noels (2022) note that there are some major psychological impacts of name change among Chinese international students, who often adopt an English name, as well as their experiences with their name mispronunciations. Piller (2016, p. 194) reports an example of an international student from South Korea who left a suicide note under her unit coordinator's office door because she was about to fail a unit at the University of Sydney. On the note, the student described herself as a 'loser' who did not have enough English to cope with her course. She felt 'guilty' that her English was not better and that she 'betrayed' her parents with her poor English and other people who cared for her. Similar cases, where international students in Australia suffer from serious psychological damages such as social withdrawal, a sense of non-belonging, low self-esteem, fear, and anxiety over using and speaking English in academic and non-academic settings, are also noted in previous studies (Dryden et al., 2021). This section will discuss some of the most common emotionality elements – the quality or state of being emotional or highly emotional (Dovchin, 2021) – caused by translingual discrimination such as foreign language anxiety and translingual inferiority complexes. Further, how trans-national migrants adopt a coping strategy by creating a positive translingual emotional safe space will also be described in this section.

4.2 Foreign Language Anxiety

One of the most common negative emotionality effects that may emerge from translingual discrimination is foreign language anxiety (FLA) – a negative emotional reaction that involves 'the feeling of tension and apprehension specifically associated with second language contexts, including speaking, listening, and learning' (MacIntyre & Gardner, 1994, p. 284). As Horwitz et al.'s (1986, p. 128) classic work on FLA suggests:

> Adults typically perceive themselves as reasonably intelligent, socially-adept individuals, sensitive to different socio-cultural mores. These assumptions are rarely challenged when communicating in a first language, as it is usually not difficult to understand others or make oneself understood. However, the situation when learning a foreign language stands in marked contrast. Because individual communication attempts will be evaluated according to uncertain and even unknown linguistic and socio-cultural standards, second language communication entails risk and is necessarily problematic.

From this perspective, FLA is a context-based anxiety reaction depending on those particular communicative situations and contexts (Horwitz et al., 1986), as even language users who are fully proficient or fluent in those particular foreign languages may suffer a great deal from the anxiety of speaking as they often compare their proficiency to that of first-language speakers (Tóth, 2010). In particular, when transnational migrants feel the elements of translingual discrimination, they start developing fear and anxiety over rejection, including the symptoms of forgetfulness, feelings of isolation, and self-avoidance, as they, for example, self-judge their own English competence and skills against native speakers of English (Dryden et al., 2021). For example, Serene (23), a migrant from South Korea who had lived in Australia for eighteen months, showed considerable manifestations of FLA in her interactions, which led to the negative emotional reactions of voicelessness and forgetfulness to such an extent that she was unable to state her feelings or experiences during a recorded focus group discussion (Dryden et al., 2021, pp. 5–7). Similarly, Khulantsetseg, a Mongolian participant in Australia, describes her experience: 'When my English is corrected by native English speakers, I start getting very anxious and not confident speaking English. I feel like my English is under strict scrutiny, and I feel not confident or motivated to speak English around them' (Interview, 22 September 2018, WA). Here, Khulantsetseg shows a classic example of FLA, in which she feels 'anxious' when her English is specifically scrutinised by native English speakers when her English is 'corrected'. Khulantsetseg's usage of English as a foreign language reduces her enthusiasm, passion, and motivation to communicate in English, consistent with previous FLA studies (Liu & Jackson, 2008).

FLA is particularly apparent in institutional settings in which the language users may have to be actively involved in expressing themselves through their foreign or second language skills. In classroom contexts (Daubney et al., 2017), for example, FLA may completely diminish one's willingness to communicate with classmates as the foreign language user may self-rate their linguistic competence as insufficient compared to their first language peers (Tóth, 2010). In fact, many international students in our study have noted that they feel FLA intensely in English-medium classrooms in Australian university contexts when they start communicating in English with peers. Many Chinese students, for example, choose to stay silent in the classroom as they get anxious about making mistakes when using English, including with the tutor. Therefore, FLA hinders foreign language users from effective intercultural and interpersonal communication, decreases peer and group solidarity or team building (Tenzer et al., 2014), impairs peer or collegial relations, and strengthens power hierarchies (Harzing & Feely, 2008).

The adverse reactions of FLA can also be physical, in which foreign language users may physically experience 'perspiration', 'sweaty palms and feet, jittery hands and feet, a dry mouth, and an increased pulse' (Aichhorn & Puck, 2017, p. 751). The physical reactions of FLA are also apparent across our research participants: Diwali (27), from the Philippines, notes, 'I'm always nervous and anxious when I speak English in Australia as I feel so intimidated by the Australian English. When I get nervous, my bottom lip starts shaking'

(Interview, 29 March 2022, WA); Zhu (20), from China, recalls, 'I often start stuttering when I'm anxious speaking English. Especially when I feel people do not really understand what I'm trying to say. I start stuttering' (Interview, 29 March 2022, WA). During our focus group discussion, Serene from South Korea manifested intense adverse physical reactions to FLA, which led to breaking down, crying, whimpering, and pause-filled utterances in English (Dryden et al., 2021, pp. 5–7).

Overall, FLA can harm the social, personal, academic, and professional interactions of transnational migrants in multiple different settings. More seriously, the devastating nature of FLA can further result in a perpetual sense of 'linguistic inferiority complexes' (Kenchappanavar, 2012) – 'the psychological and emotional damages inflicted on the victims of linguistic subordination, which result in self-marginalisation, self-vindication, loss of social belonging, social withdrawal, fear, anxiety, and the erosion of self-confidence' (Tankosić et al., 2021, p. 1785).

4.3 Translingual Inferiority Complexes

'Translingual inferiority complexes' in this Element refers to the harmful psychological, emotional, and physical damages inflicted on the victims of translingual discrimination, which lead not only to the psychological and emotional traits of self-marginalisation, self-vindication, loss of social belonging and self-confidence, and social withdrawal, but also to physical damages such as eating disorders, drug abuse, self-harm, and depression. Such damaging emotional aspects in relation to migrants' English ability stem from the homogeny of hegemonic and native English ideology and emerge once language users' linguistic abilities are rejected by others. According to Piller (2016, p. 192), linguistic inferiority complexes are directly associated with traits of linguistic subordination: 'the discourses and practices of global English bring with them their own inferiority complexes and are associated with similar psychological deformations as those noted for class and race and, in fact, all social structures of inequality'. Translingual discrimination thus often leads to the development of inferiority complexes, as it instigates feelings of being in a never-ending race to achieve the unachievable: that is, the idealised hegemonic English standard.

Translingual inferiority complexes are developed when transnational migrants' English language practices are suppressed by the host society and when they start seeing contemptible and shameful pictures of their English usage in their daily lives. Monolingual mindsets in the host society discriminate against the culture and identity of transnational migrants, which may lead to a lack of acknowledgement of their proficiency in both English and their otherlanguage(s), for example heritage or first languages. This translingual discrimination leaves them with feelings of linguistic invisibility and inferiority (Dobinson & Mercieca, 2020). Consider the example of Wang, a Chinese student in Australia, who describes his own translingual inferiority complexes when he started living in North America as a teenager (Dovchin, 2020b, p. 812). Wang started feeling subtle and overt translingual discrimination from the host society, especially when he communicated in English in Canada. Consequently, Wang started feeling a sense of non-belonging:

> that's what I felt when I was in North America. So, when you go to the grocery or whatever. I feel like you don't belong there. No sense of belonging. I was like, 'this is not the type of lifestyle I want, but I cannot walk out of it.' It just gets worse every time. It's just I just can't come up with my own thoughts. I was afraid of saying the wrong things. I was afraid of speaking out. (Dovchin, 2020b, p. 812)

Here, Wang describes his own translingual inferiority complexes, in which he feels his fear of speaking out, self-consciousness, and restriction when he speaks English, and a sense of non-belonging that comes with those complexes (Tenzer et al., 2014). These traits of self-marginalisation, self-vindication, loss of social belonging, and social withdrawal are the psychological damages resulting from FLA that arise when, according to Kenchappanavar (2012, p. 1), 'a person finds himself in a situation where his abilities and attitudes are denigrated or rejected by other people'. This is because anything in the individual that is 'below the average, that provokes unfavourable comment or gives him a feeling of impotency or ineptitude leads to inferiority complex' (Kenchappanavar, 2012, p. 1). Eventually, Wang started avoiding and withdrawing from social events and communication and became less likely to respond or fully communicate in English (Dovchin, 2020b).

Wang's situation is slightly different from that of Natasha, a woman from Ukraine who had developed paranoia because of her heavy Ukrainian accent (Table 6).

Here, Natasha explains how she felt paranoid about her work colleagues mocking her accent behind her back, but she did not confront them at the time (line 5). The scrutiny of Natasha's English accent by her co-workers made her believe that her English was 'mockable', and she started feeling unsettling experiences of paranoia that her co-workers were criticising her accent behind her back (line 3). According to previous studies, human beings are more likely to experience paranoid thoughts when they are in vulnerable, isolated, or stressful situations that could lead to them feeling negative about themselves. For example, if one is bullied at work or one's identity is attacked, it could give them suspicious thoughts, developing into paranoia (R. Lee, 2017). This is what

Table 6 Interview, 1 May 2019, WA

#	Interview transcript (in English)
1	**Natasha:** [My accent] is the way how I speak. This is basically my identity. Like who you are. And then they [referring to her Australian work colleagues] are basically like mocking you as a person.
2	**Researcher:** How?
3	**Natasha:** I had a few times in my life and I can say that was the worst experience of when someone just do it like behind your back and would not just look at my face.
4	**Researcher:** Did you confront them?
5	**Natasha:** No. I just left. If that kind of things happen, you never confront them.
6	**Researcher:** Why not?
7	**Natasha:** Because I don't know. I have a power to walk away. So, sometimes I can turn around and I can defend myself. Sometimes just leave it as it is and I forget about it. But some days I still get worse.
8	**Researcher:** Yeah?
9	**Natasha:** There was this thing happened like when they were talking behind my back. I still have a memory in my head that they were talking behind my back. So, I met them again recently. And I actually told them, you know, by the way, by that time I saw you were talking behind my back and copying my accent. They were all like no no no.

happened to Natasha as she is not able to fully prove that her co-workers were talking behind her back; as she iterates, 'Because I don't know' (line 7).

Scholars also note that inferiority complexes exaggerate normal feelings of inferiority, which may further develop into severe mental health issues such as substance abuse and eating disorders (Dovchin, 2020b; Kenchappanavar, 2012). The accumulation of translingual inferiority complexes may cause severe psychological issues, with MRI studies showing noticeable psychological and neurological impacts arising from translingual discrimination (Bhatia, 2018). Many transnational migrants in this study have stated how they have started smoking heavily and drinking alcohol (Dovchin, 2021) due to their low proficiency in English and overall communication barriers in Australia. A Mongolian-background woman, Gerel (39), who lives in Australia, explains, 'I have started drinking heavily due to my communication barrier in Australia. I was ashamed of speaking to people in English. I would just drink and smoke and cry to myself all day' (Interview, 1 August 2018, WA). The signs of eating disorders have also been apparent, as another Mongolian-background migrant woman, Altai (42), describes, 'I became very sad in Australia because I felt so worthless. I could not drive, and my English was so bad. I didn't feel self-worthy anymore outside as I was worried about my English. I started eating a lot and purged my food' (Interview, 1 August 2018, WA). This statement is consistent with recent studies in which the rise in eating disorders is noted in ethnic minorities in Western countries (Rodgers et al., 2018) due to aspects such as sudden linguistic and cultural change, and adoption of Western values and attitudes (Sussman & Truong, 2011).

The accumulation of translingual inferiority complexes may further cause severe psychological issues such as depression, paranoia, and suicidal ideations (Bhatia, 2018). A Vietnamese Australian migrant, Van (19), who was chronically bullied at school due to her Vietnamese accented English, started developing intense suicidal ideations as she started noticing herself being 'depressed'. 'I felt like I really lost in that environment. It was a time that I thought of depression. I wanted to kill myself back then … I wanted to cut myself' (Interview, 9 October 2018, WA). In a similar vein, a Chinese student, Wang (20), describes that he started developing suicidal ideation due to his sense of non-belonging: 'I even attempted suicide. I talked to another friend who had depression before, and he kind of talked me out of that. But I was already having … It was … Oh, My God! I was already ready to have a bottle of pesticide by my side' (Dovchin, 2020b, p. 813). Wang's reaction is in line with other studies (Dovchin, 2020b, 2021; Dovchin & Dryden, 2022; Rishel & Miller, 2017) which have demonstrated a direct link between the loss of a sense of belonging and suicidal ideation. Overall, translingual inferiority complexes lead to the residual mental burden of the psychological and emotional unsatisfaction of feeling not enough, massively inhibiting migrants' abilities to live their day-to-day lives, often making the quality of their life in Australia joyless, with migrants actively avoiding social situations which may require interactions in English that could lead to their linguistic subordination (Tankosić et al., 2021).

4.4 Translingual Safe Space

According to Harpalani (2017), the understanding of 'safe spaces' generally refers to either physical or social spaces which provide opportunities for socially marginalised groups to gather and discuss their daily socio-cultural problems that are not well communicated by members outside of their group. As these spaces are 'safe', they allow the participants to support each other while making emotional connections with peers who share similar circumstances (Harpalani, 2017). The term 'translingual safe space', from this view, refers to a coping strategy of transnational migrants who create an emotionally safe and positive space where they can share their negative emotionality using translingual resources. That is, deploying their full linguistic repertoire 'without regard for watchful adherence to the socially and politically defined boundaries of named (and usually national and state) languages' (Otheguy et al., 2015, p. 281). Since translingual practices allow linguistic and verbal freedom of expression, where language users can enjoy the all-fantastic dimensions of their full communicative repertoires, it maximises their communicative potential. As a result, translingual space encourages language users to seamlessly integrate linguistic resources in their communicative repertoires instead of seeking to stick to dominant standard language hegemony (Perera, 2020). Once these transnational migrants are together, they are also engaged with collaborative language production, which is often deemed as free of surveillance – 'emotionally safe spaces' as they seek out each other for consolation and emotional affinity, and spaces for emotional relief (Dovchin, 2021). Sharing a common safe space, where transnational migrants can freely express themselves linguistically and paralinguistically, helps them cope with their negative emotionality, permitting greater self-expression and positive emotions that enable a more positive and effective interactional environment (Ollerhead, 2019). As Dryden et al. (2021, p. 3) note, 'translanguaging spaces also allow for a more comfortable negotiation of meaning and identity among migrant EFL learners, in which they can share their understanding of being different on cultural, linguistic, ethnic, and/or racial grounds'. Translanguaging space is indeed a space where migrants can 'talk freely without feeling judged, stereotyped, or evaluated' as it encourages 'empathy, inclusiveness, positive emotions, and linguistic and cultural expression' (Dryden et al., 2021, p. 3). Correspondingly, it also creates an emotionally safe space, allowing transnational migrants to manage and negotiate their negative emotions and feelings related to their lived linguistic and cultural experiences in a new country (Lang, 2019).

Previous studies on translingualism have illustrated positive examples of translingual safe spaces for transnational migrants. In his detailed study, Canagarajah (2017), for instance, presents how Zimbabwean background nurses working in a UK hospital seek to conform to the English monolingual standard language requirements in the workplace. Nevertheless, these nurses also gather in a translingual safe space by engaging and interacting with other transnational background nurses. When these nurses are together, they adopt translingual practices – the available linguistic and communicative resources they have, be it English or Shona – without feeling any external pressure to use only English in its standard form. They seek to overcome their emotionality stemming from translingual discrimination through collaborative translingual production by linguistically assisting and aiding one another and emotionally conforming to each other (Canagarajah, 2017, pp. 31–2). Establishing in-group translingual space is thus deemed as free of surveillance – 'safe houses' or 'safe spaces' for these transnational nurses as they seek out each other for consolation, solace, and emotional affinity, and spaces for psychological relief. Similarly, our research participant, a Vietnamese Australian migrant, Van, who was chronically bullied at school due to her accented English, noticed that it is better to 'stay at her own level', where she started to make relationships with other people who speak English as a foreign language. As Van explains, 'I'm not talking with you [referring to English as first-language users]' (Dovchin, 2020b, p. 810). Van reveals that she was able to find relief from the interactions with other transnational migrants as they were more likely to communicate efficiently and show more respect to each other. In a group situation, translingual spaces were constructed to accommodate all listeners, help them negotiate meaning, and enable values to be shared (García-Mateus & Palmer, 2017). As Van further notes, 'we really could connect with each other and no judgement or nothing' (Interview, 9 October 2018, WA). Van's sentiment is also evident in the context of other migrants. A Mongolian-background migrant woman, Tsetseg (26), for example, explains that she finds comfort in sharing her linguistic and communicative burdens with another migrant speaker: 'I tend to understand migrants' English much better than Australians. Their English is very easy to understand, and I don't get anxious. I feel much more comfortable being around migrants than Australians as we understand each other' (Interview, 21 February 2020, WA). A translingual space for Tsetseg is, therefore, a linguistically and emotionally safe space shared with other migrants, which helps her feel comfortable and avoid anxiety and fear of speaking in English while encouraging freedom of expression, mutual understanding, and connection. Tsetseg's example is also apparent with our Ukrainian participants. They identify their comfort zone as speaking to people who are either used to translingual environments or come from non-English-speaking migrant backgrounds (Dryden et al., 2021).

A translingual safe space fosters positive emotionality, feelings of happiness and well-being, and the pleasure and joy of expressing oneself freely (Kiramba & Harris, 2019). Most Mongolian-background migrant women in Australia describe that when they are together, they seem to feel most at ease and feel happy and relaxed when they do not have to speak 'only English' with one another (Dovchin, 2019a). When translingual space was offered to Alimaa, a Mongolian-background migrant in Australia, during one of our focus group discussions, she expressed her feeling of satisfaction: 'It is so much more satisfying when we speak Mongolian, right? We don't have many opportunities anyway, right?' (Dryden et al., 2021, p. 8). Another participant, Saruul, explained that she feels much more comfortable when she hangs out with her fellow Mongolians than local Australians because their peer bond is based on their shared daily struggles and problems. As Saruul described:

> I started going to every event held by Mongolians [when she first arrived in Australia]. Like Mongolian festivals and social meetings. We would hang out, share our problems and struggles. I could speak Mongolian to them as if I was in Mongolia without any self-consciousness. I felt like I was meeting with my family in Mongolia. We used to enjoy speaking Mongolian because I really missed my country. We even use Russian [when we hang out together] because Russian is also like a native language for many Mongolians. (Interview, 7 September 2018, WA) (See also, Dovchin, 2019a, p. 343.)

To sum up, while transnational migrants are relieved of the pressure to converse in only English, more specifically in standard English as they are most accustomed to, they employ translingual repertoires created by the mixture of full linguistic repertoires available to them, be it Mongolian, English, Ukrainian, or Portuguese. This linguistically safe space not only enables them to comprehend their communication fully but also enjoy each other's company while managing their negative emotionality. Translingual safe space, therefore, is a space to empower its interactants to engage in easier resolution of language difficulties (Li, 2018) while creating an emotionally safe space that can accommodate and include all participants, help them negotiate meaning, and enable emotions to be shared (García-Mateus & Palmer, 2017). As Dryden et al. (2021, p. 3) point out, 'It may foster feelings of inclusivity and belonging . . ., allow interlocutors to connect over personal experiences . . ., and foster recognition of how language users' multiple identities overlap and are expressed in their lives.'

4.5 Conclusion

In this section, the notion of translingual discrimination has been discussed concerning transnational migrants' emotionality, as the chains of linguistically discriminative elements about one's translingual backgrounds can cause harmful impacts on one's emotionality, potentially leading to other serious mental and physical consequences. The struggles of translingual migrants who are using English as an additional language are real, as the systemic exclusion of what translingual migrants might bring to the host society leads them to live a life that risks contemplating or committing suicide, or engaging in other risky behaviours. Some of the most common negative emotionality traits caused by translingual discrimination are the notions of foreign language anxiety and translingual inferiority complexes. FLA refers to adverse emotional reactions specifically associated with the context in which the English as an additional language learner lives, in which the language learners start developing fear and anxiety about rejection based on how they speak and use the target language. Data examples show that due to the constant accumulation of translingual discriminatory experiences, many transnational migrants suffer from FLA. Their effective communication ability and motivation are reduced in that foreign language, English in this case, and their desire to communicate is grossly diminished.

More seriously, the devastating nature of FLA can further result in a perpetual sense of translingual inferiority complexes – the negative psychological and emotional consequences that are inflicted on the victims of translingual discrimination that can result in self-marginalisation, self-vindication, loss of social belonging, social withdrawal, fear, anxiety, and the erosion of self-confidence. Translingual inferiority complexes may further lead to physical damages such as eating disorders, drug abuse, self-harm, and depression. The majority of our research participants in this study have shown traits of translingual inferiority complexes, suggesting they may be carrying residual emotional and mental burdens while having permanent feelings of inferiority, weakness, and subordination, with reduced quality of life.

As a result, many transnational migrants adopt a coping strategy by creating a positive translingual emotional safe space, either a physical or social space that enables marginalised groups to gather and discuss their daily issues by deploying translingual resources – their full linguistic repertoires – without regard for watchful adherence to the socially and politically defined boundaries of the standard language. Correspondingly, a translingual safe space creates an emotionally safe and positive space where transnational migrants can share their negative emotionality and enjoy all-fantastic linguistic dimensions and full communicative potential. This collaborative translingual production is free of surveillance, creating emotionally safe spaces as transnational migrants seek out each other for consolation, emotional affinity, and spaces for emotional relief.

Based on these data findings, a recommendation is proposed for language educators and policymakers in terms of understanding translingual discrimination and its negative link to emotionality in transnational migrants' language behaviours. In order to decrease migrants' lived experience with translingual discrimination in the host society and to maximise the opportunities for them to smoothly integrate, language educators should acknowledge that these transnational migrants' emotional, psychological, and mental factors linked with translingual discrimination might hinder them from effective English language learning, and hence result in low integration into the host society (Gkonou et al., 2020).

Prolonged exposure to translingual inferiority complex and its debilitating effects such as depression, eating disorders, and substance abuse are causing chronic emotional and psychological stress to these migrants, preventing them from learning, and increasing the cycle of language-learning disruptions. Outcomes suggest a need for appropriate interventions or early preventions aimed at reducing inferiority complexes and foreign language anxiety symptoms that have the potential to negatively impact linguistic and social participation in the host society. This will bring the desired reality to migrant language policymaking decisions, which heightens the appeal of the language curriculum or programme to the migrants and consequently ensures more engagement and better English learning experience for them (Tomlinson, 2011). Understanding migrants' emotionality, therefore, may open the opportunity for language educators, social workers, psychologists, and policymakers to recognise their language-learning challenges and to understand their multiple desires, emotions, ordeals, and other associated psychological and mental burdens embedded within their multiple ways of learning, being, and speaking.

5 The Implications of Translingual Discrimination

5.1 Re-visiting Translingual Discrimination

The concept of translingual discrimination developed in this Element has enabled us to analyse language-based discrimination from its multiple layers, capturing the relations between the linguistic practices of transnational migrants and the marginalisation and exclusions they encounter, while paying equal attention to ideological and practical associations. Translingual discrimination refers to the ideologies and practices that produce unequal linguistic power relationships between minority transnational migrant-background language users and the majority population in the host society, focusing on the central role that language plays in the enduring relevance of discrimination, disparity, and exclusion (section 1). Translingual 'indexicality' (Blommaert, 2010) – registers, resources, and semiotics for transnational groups and individuals – is often ordered in hierarchies of different values and powers, institutionalised by the national order of things (section 1). As transnational migrants operate in different contexts and spaces, while often positioned in multiple unequal power settings, the sociolinguistic histories they bring with them are assigned different values, eventually becoming subject to translingual discrimination in the host society.

The understanding of translingual discrimination moves beyond two main concepts, interlingual and intralingual discrimination, as it allows a new way of looking at the language practices of transnational migrants in the current, globalised world. On the one hand, interlingual discrimination is understood through the unequal hierarchical power relationship between minority and hegemonic language groups at the level of inter-nations. Here, minority ethnic groups cannot fully utilise their mother tongues or heritage languages in critical political, linguistic, and social participation (Phillipson & Skutnabb-Kangas, 1995; Skutnabb-Kangas, 2000). For some scholars, English is a hegemonic and imperialistic language today because of substantial linguistic inequalities between English and other global languages. English-speaking Western nations, for example, use English to suppress the other non-English-speaking nations around the world, which may cause interlingual discrimination (Phillipson, 1992, 2010).

On the other hand, the concept of intralingual discrimination has been suggested as a better candidate by another group of scholars (Blommaert, 2001a, 2001b; Makoni, 2014; Wee, 2011) for an understanding of language-based discrimination, since it could be more beneficial to recognise internal language inequalities than only focusing on inter-nation language discriminations. Intralingual discrimination refers to the practices where language users may exercise control over their own languages, determining what languages are, which languages are essential, and what they may mean in that particular local context. If we understand language-based inequality through intralingual discrimination, language users of non-standard varieties of the particular standard language in that society can become potential victims (Makoni, 2012). For example, users of Singlish are potentially discriminated against due to a language policy that promotes standard English in Singapore (Wee, 2011). Intralingual discrimination is, therefore, mainly contested within an in-group space or the same linguistic and cultural groups (Blommaert, 2001a, 2001b).

Meanwhile, there is another concern that intralingual discrimination may not necessarily address current transnational superdiverse linguistic diversity and its complex transcultural and translingual entanglement with other social, ethnic, racial, gender, technological, political, economic, and ideological settings (Appadurai, 1997; Dovchin, 2018). Its primary focus on the same in-group linguistic community rights may also involve a host of exclusions such as complex, layered forms of language discrimination based on other kaleidoscopic, vernacular, pidgin, or emergent translingual practices defined by one's transnational movement (Pennycook, 2007). Just as interlingual discrimination may do little more than pluralise multilingual discrimination, intralingual discrimination does little more than pluralise monolingual discrimination (section 1).

The concept of translingual discrimination is thus introduced in this Element to capture the discrimination and exclusion emerging from one's translingual sociolinguistic background, formed by diverse transnational linguistic and semantic resources from various languages in the transgressive mixture of various codes, modes, genres, and stylisation within and beyond one's linguistic boundaries. These translingual resources do not fully become subject to discrimination through the lens of separate local and global languages but rather fall into exclusions while operating across different modalities and deploying a range of meaning-making practices across languages. As transnational migrants transgress various linguistic and semiotic modes in their daily lives, they produce new possibilities of translingual discrimination through new combinations of linguistic and cultural resources (Dovchin & Dryden, 2022). Their translingual practices also become subject to a different order of indexicality institutionalised by the national order of things – a set of general rules, traditions, and policies needed to form the nation-state (Malkki, 1995a, 1995b). Some forms of translingual indexicality can be deemed legitimate, while others can be seen as less valued, depending on the local or national context (Blommaert, 2010). In other words, standard monolingual dominant language ideologies and policies are primarily enforced on how transnationals communicate, while transnationals' translingual backgrounds only gain importance when others validate or legitimise them. What may be a gain or advantage in one context can be a total loss in another (section 1).

5.2 The Elements of Translingual Discrimination

Translingual discrimination has been unpacked in this Element through its two main characteristics – translingual name discrimination (section 2) and translingual English discrimination (section 3). Translingual name discrimination is one of the primary forms of discrimination that transnational migrants encounter in the host society, as their intrinsic qualities and skills are instantly subverted based on their birth name (Dovchin & Dryden, 2022). Because the names and naming practices of transnational migrants may present their ethnic, linguistic, and cultural identities, their birth names may often deviate from the normative naming traditions of the settlement society (section 2). As discussed in section 2, translingual name discrimination has been experienced by most of our research participants, who have transnational migrant backgrounds and are mainly settled in Australia (section 2). Tsetseg, a Mongolian participant in Australia, for example, describes in our follow-up interview: 'The first thing I did in Australia was to change my Mongolian name as I started feeling extremely shy of my name as people started having difficulties in pronouncing my name. Then I had to change my real name on my CV to a new English name, Lily, because I didn't get any calls back when I applied for jobs' (follow-up interview, 11 February 2022, WA). In this account, Tsetseg describes her experience with a particular element of translingual name discrimination that I call translingual name stigma – a collective negative stigma based on imagined or imaginary attributes associated with transnational migrants' birth names (section 2). Tsetseg's birth name has caused overall negative stigmas about her status as a 'skilled' individual. Her distinctively ethnic sounding Mongolian name, embedded at the beginning of her CV, led to no call-backs from employers. Here, Tsetseg further touches on another element of translingual name discrimination – translingual name microaggressions – the micro and subtle form of discriminatory practices against migrants' birth names such as mispronunciation, misspelling, misunderstanding, misgendering, mocking, or failing to remember migrants' birth names (section 2). As Tsetseg recalls, 'people started having difficulties in pronouncing my name' (follow-up interview, 11 February 2022, WA). As discussed in section 2, Tsetseg adopted the coping strategies of CV-whitening (Kang et al., 2016) and renaming practices (Lahiri-Roy et al., 2021), in which transnational migrants attempt to avoid anticipated labour discrimination by Anglicising or replacing their birth names with new English names and/or removing other ethnic clues when they present their CVs to employers. Evidently, Tsetseg attempted to evade translingual name stigma by whitening her CV, replacing her birth name with an English name, Lily (an approximate English translation for her Mongolian birth name, Tsetseg, which means 'flower' in English). These coping strategies, such as CV-whitening and renaming strategies (section 2), are common among transnational migrants, from Romanising one's birth name to replacing it with English names, from Chinese Bo to English Bob (section 2).

Transnational migrants' settlement journey does not end here but worsens further. The next stop is 'translingual English discrimination' – the ideologies and practices that may exclude transnational migrants from social, employment, and other opportunities based on their usage, proficiency, and practices of English (section 3). As described in section 3, translingual English discrimination has its own elements, such as accentism and translingual stereotyping and hallucination. Translingual English accentism refers to the ideologies and practices that discriminate against transnational migrants' biographical English accents in favour of standard-English accents (Dryden & Dovchin, 2021; Lippi-Green, 2011). Accentism was a shared lived experience for many research participants. For instance, Oksana (35), from Ukraine, described, 'I had to deal with my English accent from scratch as I started getting a lot of corrections, light jokes and even mocking about my accent' (interview, 1 May 2019, WA). While accentism may occur in both overt and covert forms, in Oksana's experience, she encountered a covert form of accentism – a subtle way of discriminating against a person's accent through corrections, mockery, and subtle jokes (section 3).

Another research participant, an Australian-born, Chinese-background participant, Zhu (20), explains in our follow-up conversation:

> English is my first language. In fact, my Chinese is not that great. But I have been told all my life how good my English is for someone who is from China. Even Chinese people come to me and start talking to me in Chinese because they think my first language is Chinese or my English is not good or something like that. (Interview, 14 February 2022, WA)

Here, Zhu's account helps us unpack another element of translingual English discrimination, translingual English stereotyping and hallucination – the pre-fixed, stereotypical view that transnational migrants' English proficiency will be low, irrespective of their actual fluent English proficiency, purely based on how they look (e.g., their skin colour, race, or ethnic garments) (Dovchin, 2020b; Fought, 2006). Despite English being Zhu's first language, she still encounters translingual English stereotyping due to her 'Chinese' look. Accent hallucination could also be a factor here, as native English speakers may hear a 'Chinese' accent that is non-existent when Zhu presents as 'non-Anglo' (section 3).

In section 3, I further discuss how transnational migrants seek to resist translingual discrimination by adopting specific coping strategies. Tsetseg, from Mongolia, has adopted a strategy called purification – the effort to reduce one's biographical English accent and pronunciation to acquire a 'proper' English accent (Dovchin, 2019a). This effort includes the rigorous drilling and practising of one's accent, as Diwali from the Philippines, for example, explains: 'Of course, I work on my accent every day. I listen to how my husband talks to his friends, and I mimic him sometimes. He helps me to learn a proper Aussie accent' (follow-up interview, 11 February 2022, WA). Here, Diwali refers to her Australian husband and his Australian accent, as she seeks to purify her Filipino accent through practising with her husband. Many transnational migrants in this study also adopt a coping strategy of ethnic evasion, that is, avoiding their linguistic and cultural groups or avoiding using their first languages (Dovchin, 2019a). As Tsetseg from Mongolia explains, 'I often avoid speaking Mongolian to my kids as I want them to learn English properly' (follow-up interview, 11 February 2022, WA). Tsetseg further notes that she avoids hanging out with Mongolians or other Mongolian community-based events in Australia to expand her effort 'to become a proper Australian' (interview, 11 February 2022, WA).

Due to the accumulation of all these elements of translingual discrimination, most research participants in this study have expressed their negative emotionality, which was discussed in section 4. Many transnational migrants have expressed the emotional damage and psychological traumas they experienced in dealing with elements of translingual discrimination. For example, foreign language anxiety (Horwitz et al., 1986) – adverse emotional reactions in which foreign language learners develop fear and anxiety of rejection based on how they speak and use the target language – was common among the research participants (section 4). As Oksana from Ukraine notes, 'Yes, I'm always anxious and nervous when I speak English. It is one of my largest fears' (interview, 1 May 2019, WA). As explained in section 4, foreign language anxiety is also a direct consequence of translingual inferiority complexes (Tankosić et al., 2021) – the negative psychological and emotional consequences that are inflicted on the victims of translingual discrimination, which may result in self-marginalisation, self-vindication, loss of social belonging, social withdrawal, and the erosion of self-confidence (Kenchappanavar, 2012). As Van from Vietnam, who suffered from accentism during her schooling, points out, 'I always feel like a second citizen because my background is Vietnamese. I don't have a full sense of belonging in Australia, and I'm not a confident person at all. I never feel my English is enough' (interview, 9 October 2018, WA). Like Van, many research participants in this study have shown the traits of translingual inferiority complexes, carrying the residual emotional and mental burdens while having permanent feelings of inferiority, weakness, and subordination, with a reduced quality of life. More severely, some of the migrants suffered from severe mental and physical issues such as depression, suicidal thoughts, self-harm, eating disorders, and drug abuse (section 4). Nevertheless, to combat these negative emotionalities, as highlighted in section 4, many migrants adopt a coping strategy of establishing translingual emotional safe spaces – in-group spaces where migrants hang out together, using their full linguistic repertoires without regard for watchful adherence to named languages as they seek out each other for consolation, emotional affinity, and spaces for emotional relief (Canagarajah, 2017; Canagarajah & Dovchin, 2019; Dryden et al., 2021). As Zhu from China, for example, notes, 'I enjoy hanging out with other immigrants a lot because we understand each other's problems' (interview, 14 February 2022, WA).

5.3 The Social Implications of Translingual Discrimination

From the position I have been developing in this Element, language-based discrimination starts to be seen not so much in terms of interlingual or intralingual systems but in terms of one's sociolinguistic history, background, and identity practices. We can start to view language-based discrimination as translingual discrimination: that is, discrimination based on one's multimodal semiotics and linguistic resourcefulness (Pennycook, 2012), whose linguistic practices have been crafted by their life-long lived experiences. When migrants move to a new environment, they engage in communicative processes through a variety of resources available to them, including both local and translocal identity attributes. Yet, they become subject to discrimination and marginalisation due to the prescriptive unilateral relationship between the exocentric monolithic norm of language (e.g., English) and the unconventional and non-normative usage of that host nation's language. For example, once the existing linguistic practices of transnational migrants in Australia have been found translingual, that is, socially unorthodox and hence socially unacceptable by the national order of things, their linguistic repertoire and sociolinguistic background could immediately define their social situation as disadvantaged (Goffman, 1963; Izadi, 2020). Therefore, instead of transnational migrants being valued as skilled and talented groups, their English features can be viewed through a deficit lens – rendering them an individual not suitable, for example, for the job on offer. This translingual invalidation shows the fragility of the situations that many transnational migrants face in their social lives in Australia and beyond, despite all the skills that transnational migrants bring to the fore. Their communication styles, which may expose their other English varieties, lead to social classification (Block, 2013), which can cause significant hurdles and barriers in the daily lives of transnational migrants when they participate in social life (Dovchin & Dryden, 2022).

Translingual discrimination leaves a final point for social implications. While it is far too easy to condemn translingual discrimination, the point that needs to be made is graver than that. It is ultimately about the inequalities between the unyielding national order of things that judge transnational migrants based on the established homogeneity and space or context where migrants do not correspond to the classifications of such orders. The first step in maintaining an inclusive multicultural society is, therefore, to start respecting transnational migrants' translingual identities, practices, backgrounds, and repertoires, including their birth names, accents, heritage languages, race, skin colour, and ethnicity. It is crucial to raise public awareness that social justice, diversity, and inclusion start from recognising migrants' biographical trajectories and their real-life achievements (Wang & Dovchin, 2022). Transnational migrants' language and communication need to be seen as part of a broader mobilisation of semiotic resources: they use a range of devices to communicate and are not necessarily reliant on people speaking the 'same' language. Policymakers should consider a current linguistic policy that prepares national institutions for 'foreign-sounding' names, and 'non-normative English' or accents as non-pragmatic issues that are just surface features that do not necessarily correspond to migrants' intrinsic values, identities, talents, skills, and competence. We, as language educators, therefore need to consider critical social implications and raise people's intercultural awareness (Baker & Fang, 2021), such as how transnational migrants may use diverse linguistic repertoires outside institutional settings, who they are, what they do, their sociolinguistic histories and backgrounds, and their multiple emotions, metapragmatic awareness, and intercultural competence (McConachy & Liddicoat, 2016) of learning, being, and speaking. In other words, we need to question the ways we talk about languages, bilingualism, and multilingualism, and think instead of translingualism as advantageous rather than damaging.

5.4 The Pedagogical Implications of Translingual Discrimination

Educators bring a considerable responsibility in influencing the views and minds of their students. This power should be treated with care. They are in a powerful position to, for example, create positive classroom environments that promote social inclusion and cultural diversity. For this reason, educators also have the resources and capacity to proactively minimise the harm of translingual discrimination in the classroom by introducing subjects of culturally relevant pedagogy and empowering migrant students' cultures and languages through multicultural resources (Kohli & Solórzano, 2012). In so doing, it is critical that we as educators identify, recognise, and expand our own cultural and linguistic awareness, as we continuously develop our efforts in learning more about different cultures and languages, despite how far it might take us outside our comfort zone. For example, the elements of translingual discrimination in this Element prove that an Anglocentric bias in all aspects of social life in Australia, including classrooms, is evident, which is primarily mandated by national standards, monolingual policies, and curriculum (Kohli & Solórzano, 2012). As educators, we should remind ourselves that elements of translingual discrimination may occur in our classrooms. Hence, it is always useful to introduce linguistically and culturally sensitive and respectful content and resources to our classrooms. We must be aware that something even as simple as saying a name incorrectly in class may lead to a snowballing of negative effects not only for migrant students but also for all participants in the classroom (section 2). It is clear that the consequences of even subtle forms of translingual discrimination are real and may have a lasting harmful impact on the well-being and self-perceptions of our students. If we therefore seek to create inclusive classrooms advocating, for example, translanguaging practices that celebrate differences and diversity in our students' learning experiences, they will maintain and develop pride in their language and culture (Tian et al., 2020). A translingual approach to education should emerge in the space between the language education policy imposed upon teachers and the actual language practices and the lived experiences of their students (Lau & Van Viegen, 2020). This is a relationship that must be signified if we are to provide students with an equitable education (García & Kleyn, 2016). This will bring a desired reality to language policymaking decisions, heightening the appeal of the multilingual curriculum or programme to migrants and consequently ensuring more engagement and better English language acquisition for them (Seals & Olsen-Reeder, 2019). Promoting translanguaging practice in language education can build awareness and valuing of students' language practices and skills, while boosting their engagement, motivation, metalinguistic awareness, comprehension, and positive identity construction.

In addition, as discussed in section 4, prolonged exposure to foreign language anxiety and translingual inferiority complexes caused by the elements of translingual discrimination may cause chronic mental and physical harm to transnational migrants (Dovchin, 2021). Within the migrant community, there is a high prevalence of mental health issues due to immigration stressors such as loss of sense of belonging, the processes of acculturation and citizenship, gaining employment and finances, and language and literacy (Fortuna et al., 2016). A further recommendation is thus proposed for language educators, particularly intercultural communication and TESOL educators, in the host society in terms of understanding translingual discrimination and its link to emotionality in our migrant-background students' language behaviours (Dovchin, 2021). To maximise the opportunities for our students to smoothly integrate into a new English-dominant society like Australia, the USA or the UK, language educators should develop a better understanding in terms of migrants' emotional, psychological, and mental factors, as these factors could prevent migrants from obtaining effective English language learning practices, and hence foster low linguistic integration into the host society (Gkonou et al., 2020). We, as language educators, must therefore play a critical role in recognising the symptoms of emotional and psychological difficulties that migrants are experiencing and take them seriously at any pedagogical level. There is a significant barrier for migrants to communicate with service providers and others about their distress and suicidality (Brown et al., 2019). Proper intervention and guidance from educators can, to a great extent, facilitate migrants' overall communication in the host society, which in turn can help maximise the results of their meaningful English learning practices. What is equally important for language and TESOL educators is to acknowledge that English language learning practices can often be contributing factors to migrants' anxiety and negative emotionality. As such, language educators should become aware of how to put migrants in contact with professional help and make recommendations to their students in an appropriate and ethical manner (Dovchin, 2021). Appropriate interventions or early preventions aimed at reducing migrants' inferiority complexes or foreign language anxiety symptoms that have the potential to negatively impact their English learning practices should be facilitated. Educators in English programmes themselves should not be completely oblivious to the practical intercultural challenges faced by their migrant students (Baker, 2015; McConachy, 2018), as these students should be provided with resources on psychological counselling, therapeutic services, and other varieties of social events that may play an essential part in boosting students' English communicative competence. As Dovchin (2021, p. 860) suggests, 'During TESOL programmes, any party involved can contribute to its effectiveness by being more cooperative and sensitive to students' emotional needs and difficulties, which will, in turn, make the environment more holistic to learning and educational exchange.' This Element concludes that transnational migrants, including our migrant-background students, deserve to experience education within a positive space that validates and advocates their language, culture, and identity. I hope that this Element will raise awareness and expand knowledge to motivate our language educators to be mindful that the consequences of even subtle forms of translingual discrimination are real and may have a lasting harmful impact on the well-being and self-perceptions of our students.

Appendix

Participants' Demographic Information

#	Pseudonym	Age	Gender	Ethnicity	Languages	Job	Years living in Australia
1.	Saruul	35	Female	Mongolian	Mongolian, English	Housewife	15
2.	Bolortsetseg Amgalanbaatar	34	Female	Mongolian	Mongolian, English	Housewife, former international student	16
3.	Tserenkhand Luvsanjantsan	59	Female	Mongolian	Mongolian, English	Housewife with degree in business management	20
4.	Khulantsetseg	27	Female	Mongolian	Mongolian, English	International student	1.5
5.	Gerel	39	Female	Mongolian	Mongolian, English, Russian	Housewife	6
6.	Tsetseg	26	Female	Mongolian	Mongolian, English	Kitchenhand	5
7.	Altantulkhuur	36	Female	Mongolian	Mongolian, English, Russian	International student	1
8.	Narangerel	36	Female	Mongolian	Mongolian, English	Housewife	15
9.	Chimeg	40	Female	Mongolian	Mongolian, English, Russian	International student	2

(cont.)

#	Pseudonym	Age	Gender	Ethnicity	Languages	Job	Years living in Australia
10.	Bolor	34	Female	Mongolian	Mongolian, English, Russian	Housewife	16
11.	Khulan	27	Female	Mongolian	Mongolian, English,	TAFE (technical and further education) student/housewife	1.5
12.	Narangerel	42	Female	Mongolian	Mongolian, English	Housewife	5
13.	Dorj	21	Male	Mongolian	Mongolian, English, Kazakh	International student	2
14.	Serene	23	Female	South Korean	Korean, English	Aged carer/cleaner	1.5
15.	Van	19	Female	Vietnamese	Vietnamese, English	Undergraduate student	5
16.	Wang	20	Male	Chinese	Chinese, English	Undergraduate student	6 months
17.	Zhu	20	Female	Chinese	Chinese, English	Undergraduate student	8 months
18.	Zhang	19	Female	Chinese	Chinese, English	Undergraduate student	1

#	Name	Age	Gender	Languages	Ethnicity	Occupation	
19.	Nadya	35	Female	Ukrainian, Russian	Ukrainian	Childcare assistant	9
20.	Natasha	51	Female	Ukrainian, Russian	Ukrainian	Housewife in Australia. PhD degree in social psychology from Ukraine	6
21.	Oksana	35	Female	Ukrainian, Russian	Ukrainian	Childcare assistant	9
22.	Ilhan	25	Female	English, Somali	Somalian New Zealander	Student and motivational speaker	5
23.	Chopra	21	Male	English	Indian, Australian	Undergraduate student	Born in Australia
24.	Diwali	27	Female	Philippines	Tagalog, English	Housewife	6

References

Aichhorn, N., & Puck, J. (2017). "I just don't feel comfortable speaking English": Foreign language anxiety as a catalyst for spoken-language barriers in MNCs. *International Business Review, 26*(4), 749–63. https://doi.org/10.1016/j.ibusrev.2017.01.004.

Allasino, E., Reyneri, E., Venturini, A., & Zincone, G. (2004). *Labour market discrimination against migrant workers in Italy.* International Labour Organization.

Appadurai, A. (1997). *Modernity at large: Cultural dimensions of globalization.* University of Minnesota Press.

Baker, W. (2015). *Culture and identity through English as a lingua franca: Rethinking concepts and goals in intercultural communication.* De Gruyter Mouton.

Baker, W., & Fang, F. (2021). "So maybe I'm a global citizen": Developing intercultural citizenship in English medium education. *Language, Culture and Curriculum, 34*(1), 1–17. https://doi.org/10.1080/07908318.2020.1748045.

Barrett, T. (2019). Transgrammaring bilinguals and "ordinary" English in Japanese ethnic churchscapes. In T. A. Barrett & S. Dovchin (Eds.), *Critical inquiries in the sociolinguistics of globalization* (pp. 119–46). Multilingual Matters.

Barrett, T. (2020). *A sociolinguistic view of a Japanese ethnic church community.* Routledge.

Bhabha, H. K. (1994). *The location of culture.* Routledge.

Bhatia, T. K. (2018). Accent, intelligibility, mental health, and trauma. *World Englishes, 37*(3), 421–31.

Block, D. (2013). *Social class in applied linguistics.* Routledge.

Blommaert, J. (2001a). The Asmara Declaration as a sociolinguistic problem: Reflections on scholarship and linguistic rights. *Journal of Sociolinguistics, 5*(1), 131–42.

Blommaert, J. (2001b). Review. Linguistic genocide in education – or worldwide diversity and human rights? T Skutnabb-Kangas. *Applied Linguistics, 22*(4), 539–41.

Blommaert, J. (2009). A market of accents. *Language Policy, 8*(3), 243–59.

Blommaert, J. (2010). *The sociolinguistics of globalization.* Cambridge University Press.

Blommaert, J., & Dong. J. (2010). *Ethnographic fieldwork: A beginner's guide.* Multilingual Matters.

Blommaert, J., & Rampton, B. (2011). Language and superdiversity. *Diversities, 13*(2), 1–22.

Bradley, J., Moore, E., Simpson, J., & Atkinson, L. (2018). Translanguaging space and creative activity: Theorising collaborative arts-based learning. *Language and Intercultural Communication, 18*(1), 54–73.

Brown, F. L., Mishra, T., Frounfelker, R. L., et al. (2019). "Hiding their troubles": A qualitative exploration of suicide in Bhutanese refugees in the USA. *Global Mental Health, 6.* https://doi.org/10.1017/gmh.2018.34.

Busetta, G., Campolo, M. G., & Panarello, D. (2018). Immigrants and Italian labor market: Statistical or taste-based discrimination? *Genus, 74*(4), 1–20. https://doi.org/10.1186/s41118-018-0030-1.

Canagarajah, S. (2013). *Translingual practice: Global Englishes and cosmopolitan relations.* Routledge.

Canagarajah, S. (2017). *Translingual practices and neoliberal policies: Attitudes and strategies of African skilled migrants in anglophone workplaces.* Springer.

Canagarajah, S. (2018). Translingual practice as spatial repertoires: Expanding the paradigm beyond structuralist orientations. *Applied Linguistics, 39*(1), 31–54.

Canagarajah, S., & Dovchin, S. (2019). The everyday politics of translingualism as a resistant practice. *International Journal of Multilingualism, 16*(2), 127–44.

Cho, G., Shin, F., & Krashen, S. (2004). What do we know about heritage languages? What do we need to know about them? *Multicultural Education, 11*(4), 23–6.

Clément, R., & Gardner, R. (2001). Second language mastery. In W. P. Robinson & H. Giles (Eds.), *The new handbook of language and social psychology* (pp. 489–504). Wiley.

Coates, K., & Carr, S. C. (2005). Skilled immigrants and selection bias: A theory-based field study from New Zealand. *International Journal of Intercultural Relations, 29*(5), 577–99.

Copland, F., & Creese, A. (2015). *Linguistic ethnography: Collecting, analysing and presenting data.* Sage.

Corona, V., & Block, D. (2020). Raciolinguistic micro-aggressions in the school stories of immigrant adolescents in Barcelona: A challenge to the notion of Spanish exceptionalism? *International Journal of Bilingual Education and Bilingualism, 23*(7), 778–88.

Creese, A., & Blackledge, A. (2010). Translanguaging in the bilingual classroom: A pedagogy for learning and teaching? *The Modern Language Journal, 94*(1), 103–15.

Creese, G., & Kambere, E. N. (2003). What colour is your English? *Canadian Review of Sociology/Revue Canadienne de Sociologie, 40*(5), 565–73.

Darvin, R., & Norton, B. (2014). Social class, identity, and migrant students. *Journal of Language, Identity & Education, 13*(2), 111–17.

Daubney, M., Dewaele, J.-M., & Gkonou, C. (2017). Introduction. In C. Gkonou, M. Daubney, & J.-M. Dewaele (Eds.), *New insights into language anxiety: Theory, research and educational implications* (pp.1–11). Multilingual Matters.

De Costa, P. I. (2020). Linguistic racism: Its negative effects and why we need to contest it. *International Journal of Bilingual Education and Bilingualism, 23*(7), 833–7.

De Klerk, V., & Bosch, B. (1995). Linguistic stereotypes: Nice accent – nice person? *International Journal of the Sociology of Language, 116*(1), 17–38.

Dewilde, J., & Creese, A. (2016). Discursive shadowing in linguistic ethnography. Situated practices and circulating discourses in multilingual schools. *Anthropology & Education Quarterly, 47*(3), 329–39.

Diao, W. (2014). Between ethnic and English names: Name choice for transnational Chinese students in a US academic community. *Journal of International Students, 4*(3),205–22.

Dick, C. (2011). *The perils of identity: Group rights and the politics of intragroup difference.* University of British Columbia Press.

Dobinson, T., & Mercieca, P. (2020). Seeing things as they are, not just as we are: Investigating linguistic racism on an Australian university campus. *International Journal of Bilingual Education and Bilingualism, 23*(7), 789–803.

Dovchin, S. (2018). *Language, media and globalization in the periphery: The linguascapes of popular music in Mongolia.* Routledge.

Dovchin, S. (2019a). Language crossing and linguistic racism: Mongolian immigrant women in Australia. *Journal of Multicultural Discourses, 14*(4), 334–51. https://doi.org/10.1080/17447143.2019.1566345.

Dovchin, S. (2019b). The politics of injustice in translingualism: Linguistic discrimination. In T. A. Barrett & S. Dovchin (Eds.), *Critical inquiries in the studies of sociolinguistics of globalization* (pp. 84–101). Multilingual Matters.

Dovchin, S. (2020a). Introduction to special issue: Linguistic racism. *International Journal of Bilingual Education and Bilingualism, 23*(7), 773–5.

Dovchin, S. (2020b). The psychological damages of linguistic racism and international students in Australia. *International Journal of Bilingual Education and Bilingualism*, *23*(7), 804–15.

Dovchin, S. (2021). Translanguaging, emotionality, and English as a second language immigrants: Mongolian background women in Australia. *TESOL Quarterly*, *55*(3), 839–65.

Dovchin, S., & Dryden, S. (2022). Translingual discrimination: Skilled transnational migrants in the labour market of Australia. *Applied Linguistics*, *43*(2), 365–88.

Dovchin, S., & Dryden, S. (2022). Unequal English accents, covert accentism and EAL migrants in Australia. International Journal of the Sociology of Language, 2022(277), 33–46.

Dovchin, S., Pennycook, A., & Sultana, S. (2017). *Popular culture, voice and linguistic diversity: Young adults on- and offline.* Springer.

Dovchin, S., Sultana, S., & Pennycook, A. (2016). Unequal translingual Englishes in the Asian peripheries. *Asian Englishes*, *18*(2), 92–108.

Dryden, S., & Dovchin, S. (2021). Accentism: English LX users of migrant background in Australia. *Journal of Multilingual and Multicultural Development*, 1–13. https://doi.org/10.1080/01434632.2021.1980573.

Dryden, S., Tankosić, A., & Dovchin, S. (2021). Foreign language anxiety and translanguaging as an emotional safe space: Migrant English as a foreign language learners in Australia. *System*, *101*, 102593.

Edo, A., Jacquemet, N., & Yannelis, C. (2019). Language skills and homophilous hiring discrimination: Evidence from gender and racially differentiated applications. *Review of Economics of the Household*, *17*(1), 349–76.

Fang, F. (2020). *Re-positioning accent attitude in the global Englishes paradigm: A critical phenomenological case study in the Chinese context.* Routledge.

Fang, F., & Liu, Y. (2020). "Using all English is not always meaningful": Stakeholders' perspectives on the use of and attitudes towards translanguaging at a Chinese university. *Lingua*, *247*, 102959. https://doi.org/10.1016/j.lingua.2020.102959.

Flores, N., & Rosa. J. (2015). Undoing appropriateness: Raciolinguistic ideologies and language diversity in education. *Harvard Educational Review*, *85*(2), 149–71.

Foo, A. L., & Tan, Y. Y. (2019). Linguistic insecurity and the linguistic ownership of English among Singaporean Chinese. *World Englishes*, *38*(4), 606–29.

Fortuna, L. R., Álvarez, K., Ortiz, Z. R., et al. (2016). Mental health, migration stressors and suicidal ideation among Latino immigrants in Spain and the United States. *European Psychiatry*, *36*, 15–22.

Foucault, M. (1988). Technologies of the self. In L. H. Martin, H. Gutman, & P. H. Hutton, (Eds.), *Technologies of the self* (pp. 16–49). The University of Massachusetts Press.

Fought, C. (2006). *Language and ethnicity.* Cambridge University Press.

Fox, S., & Stallworth, L. E. (2005). Racial/ethnic bullying: Exploring links between bullying and racism in the US workplace. *Journal of Vocational Behavior, 66*(3), 438–56.

García, O., & Kleyn, T. (2016). A translanguaging education policy: Disruptions and creating spaces of possibility. In O. García & T. Kleyn (Eds.), *Translanguaging with multilingual students: Learning from class-room moments* (pp. 181–201). Routledge.

García-Mateus, S., & Palmer, D. (2017). Translanguaging pedagogies for positive identities in two-way dual language bilingual education. *Journal of Language, Identity and Education, 16*(4), 245–55. https://doi.org/10.1080/15348458.2017.1329016.

Gkonou, C., Dewaele, J.-M., & King, J. (Eds.) (2020). *The emotional roll-ercoaster of language teaching.* Multilingual Matters.

Goffman, E. (1963). *Stigma: Notes on the management of spoiled identity.* Simon and Schuster.

Hamer, S. (2021). Colour blind: Investigating the racial bias of virtual reference services in English academic libraries. *The Journal of Academic Librarianship, 47*(5), 102416.

Hanish, L. D., & Guerra, N. G. (2000). The roles of ethnicity and school context in predicting children's victimization by peers. *American Journal of Community Psychology, 28*(2), 201–23. https://doi.org/10.1023/A:1005187201519.

Harpalani, V. (2017). "Safe spaces" and the educational benefits of diversity. *Duke Journal of Constitutional Law and Public Policy, 13*(1), 117–66.

Harzing, A. W., & Feely, A. J. (2008). The language barrier and its implications for HQ-subsidiary relationships. *Cross Cultural Management: International Journal, 15*(1), 49–61. https://doi.org/10.1108/13527600810848827.

Hawkins, M. R., & Mori, J. (2018). Considering "trans-" perspectives in language theories and practices. *Applied Linguistics, 39*(1), 1–8.

Heller, M., & McElhinny, B. (2017). *Language, capitalism, colonialism: Toward a critical history.* University of Toronto Press.

Horwitz, E. K., Horwitz, M. B., & Cope, J. (1986). Foreign language classroom anxiety. *The Modern Language Journal, 70*(2), 125–32.

Hsu, F. (2020). The "native English speaker" as Indigenous replacement: California English learner classification policies and settler grammar expressions of immigrant nationhood. *Educational Studies, 56*(3), 233–47.

Izadi, D. (2020). *The spatial and temporal dimensions of interactions.* Springer.

Jacquemet, M. (2013). Transidioma and asylum: Gumperz's legacy in intercultural institutional talk. *Journal of Linguistic Anthropology, 23*(3), 199–212.

Jamieson, A. (2018). Coronial investigation into the death of Zhikai Liu. Coroners Court of Victoria. https://bit.ly/3Sg5KEF.

Jenkins, J. (2007). *English as a lingua franca: Attitude and identity.* Oxford University Press.

Jenkins, J., & Mauranen, A. (Eds) (2019). *Linguistic diversity on the EMI campus: Insider accounts of the use of English and other languages in universities within Asia, Australasia, and Europe.* Routledge.

Kang, S. K., DeCelles, K. A., Tilcsik, A., et al. (2016). Whitened résumés: Race and self-presentation in the labor market. *Administrative Science Quarterly, 61*(3), 469–502.

Kenchappanavar, R. N. (2012). Relationship between inferiority complex and frustration in adolescents. *IOSR Journal of Humanities and Social Science, 2*(2), 1–5.

Khvorostianov, N., & Remennick, L. (2017). "By helping others, we helped ourselves": Volunteering and social integration of ex-Soviet immigrants in Israel. *Voluntas, 28*(1), 335–57.

Kiramba, L. K., & Harris, V. J. (2019). Navigating authoritative discourses in a multilingual classroom: Conversations with policy and practice. *TESOL Quarterly, 53*(2), 456–81. https://doi.org/10.1002/tesq.493.

Kohli, R., & Solórzano, D. G. (2012). Teachers, please learn our names!: Racial microaggressions and the K-12 classroom. *Race Ethnicity and Education, 15*(4), 441–62.

Kramsch, C. (2006). Preview article: The multilingual subject. *International Journal of Applied Linguistics, 16*(1), 97–110.

Kubota, R. (2015). Inequalities of Englishes, English speakers, and languages: A critical perspective on pluralist approaches to English. In R. Tupas (Ed.), *Unequal Englishes: The politics of Englishes today* (pp. 21–42). Palgrave Macmillan.

Kumaravadivelu, B. (2016). The decolonial option in English teaching: Can the subaltern act? *TESOL Quarterly, 50*(1), 66–85.

Lahiri-Roy, R., Belford, N., & Sum, N. (2021). Transnational women academics of colour enacting "pedagogy of discomfort": Positionality against a "pedagogy of rupture". *Pedagogy, Culture & Society,* 1–19. https://doi.org/10.1080/14681366.2021.1900345.

Lang, N. W. (2019). Teachers' translanguaging practices and "safe spaces" for adolescent newcomers: Toward alternative visions. *Bilingual Research Journal, 42*(1), 73–89. https://doi.org/10.1080/15235882.2018.1561550.

Lau, S. M. C., & Van Viegen, S. (Eds.) (2020). *Plurilingual pedagogies: Critical and creative endeavors for equitable language in education.* Springer.

Lee, J. W. (2017). *The politics of translingualism: After Englishes.* Routledge.

Lee, J. W. (2022). *Locating translingualism.* Cambridge University Press.

Lee, J. W., & Dovchin, S. (Eds.) (2019). *Translinguistics: Negotiating innovation and ordinariness.* Routledge.

Lee, R. J. (2017). Mistrustful and misunderstood: A review of paranoid personality disorder. *Current Behavioral Neuroscience Reports, 4*(2), 151–65.

Lee, S. J., Wong, N.-W. A., and Alvarez, A. N. (2009). The model minority and the perpetual foreigner: Stereotypes of Asian Americans. In N. Tewari and A. N. Alvarez (Eds.), *Asian American psychology: Current perspectives* (pp. 69–84). Routledge/Taylor & Francis Group.

Leng, H. (2005). Chinese cultural schema of education: Implications for communication between Chinese students and Australian educators. *Issues in Educational Research, 15*(1), 17–36.

Li, M., & Campbell, J. (2009). Accessing employment: Challenges faced by non-native English-speaking professional migrants. *Asian and Pacific Migration Journal 18*(3), 371–95.

Li, W. (2018). Translanguaging as a practical theory of language. *Applied Linguistics, 39*(1), 9–30.

Li, W., & Zhu, H. (2019). Tranßcripting: Playful subversion with Chinese characters. *International Journal of Multilingualism, 16*(2), 145–61.

Li, W., Tsang, A., Wong, N., et al. (2020). Kongish daily: Researching translanguaging creativity and subversiveness. *International Journal of Multilingualism, 17*(3), 309–35.

Lippi-Green, R. (2011). *English with an accent: Language, ideology and discrimination in the United States.* Routledge.

Liu, M., & Jackson, J. (2008). An exploration of Chinese EFL learners' unwillingness to communicate and foreign language anxiety. *The Modern Language Journal, 92*(1), 71–86. https://doi.org/10.1111/j.1540-4781.2008.00687.x.

Löfgren, O. (1989). The nationalization of culture. *Ethnologia Europaea, 19*(1), 5–24.

Lytra, V. (2008). Playful talk, learners' play frames and the construction of identities. In M. Martin-Jones, A. M. de Mejia, & N. H. Hornberger (Eds.), *Encyclopedia of language and education, 2nd Edition, Volume 3: Discourse and education* (pp. 185–97). Springer.

MacIntyre, P. D., & Gardner, R. C. (1994). The subtle effects of language anxiety on cognitive processing in the second language. *Language Learning, 44*(2), 283–305.

Makoni, S. B. (2012). Language and human rights discourses in Africa: Lessons from the African experience. *Journal of Multicultural Discourses, 7*(1), 1–20.

Makoni, S. B. (2014). Feminising linguistic human rights: Use of isihlonipho sabafazi in the courtroom and intra-group linguistic differences. *Journal of Multicultural Discourses, 9*(1), 27–43.

Malkki, L. H. (1995a). Refugees and exile: From "refugee studies" to the national order of things. *Annual Review of Anthropology, 24*(1), 495–523.

Malkki, L. H. (1995b). *Purity and exile: Violence, memory, and national cosmology among Hutu refugees in Tanzania.* University of Chicago Press.

Marzluf, P., & Saruul-Erdene, M. (2019). Mongolia: Language education policy. In A. Kirkpatrick & A. J. Liddicoat (Eds.), *The Routledge international handbook of language education policy in Asia* (pp. 137–50). Routledge.

McConachy, T. (2018). *Developing intercultural perspectives on language use: Exploring pragmatics and culture in foreign language learning.* Multilingual Matters.

McConachy, T., & Liddicoat, A. J. (2016). Meta-pragmatic awareness and intercultural competence: The role of reflection and interpretation in intercultural mediation. In F. Dervin & Z. Gross (Eds.), *Intercultural competence in education: Alternative approaches for different times* (pp. 13–30). Palgrave Macmillan.

Milroy, J., & Milroy, L. (2012). *Authority in language: Investigating standard English.* Routledge.

Munro, M. J., Derwing, T. M., & Sato, K. (2006). Salient accents, covert attitudes: Consciousness-raising for pre-service second language teachers. *Prospect, 21*(1), 67–79.

Mufwene, S. S. (2002). Colonisation, globalisation and the plight of "weak" languages. *Journal of Linguistics, 38*(2), 375–95.

Nelson, L. R., Signorella, M. L., and Botti, K. G. (2016). Accent, gender, and perceived competence. *Hispanic Journal of Behavioral Sciences, 38*(2), 166–85.

Ollerhead, S. (2019). Teaching across semiotic modes with multilingual learners: Translanguaging in an Australian classroom. *Language and Education, 33*(2), 106–22. https://doi.org/10.1080/09500782.2018.1516780.

Olson, R. (2020). *Romeo and Juliet: A textbook edition of shakespeare's play created by students, for students.* Oregon State University.

Orellana, M., Ek, L., & Hernandez, A. (1999). Bilingual education in an immigrant community: Proposition 227 in California. *International Journal of Bilingual Education and Bilingualism, 2*(2), 114–30.

Oreopoulos, P. (2011). Why do skilled immigrants struggle in the labor market? A field experiment with thirteen thousand resumes. *American Economic Journal: Economic Policy, 3*(4), 148–71.

Otheguy, R., García, O., & Reid, W. (2015). Clarifying translanguaging and deconstructing named languages: A perspective from linguistics. *Applied Linguistics Review, 6*(3), 281–307.

Palsson, G. (2014). Personal names. *Science, Technology, & Human Values, 39*(4), 618–30. https://doi.org/10.1177/0162243913516808.

Pan, L. (2015). *English as a global language in China*. Springer.

Pennycook, A. (2007). *Global Englishes and transcultural flows*. Routledge.

Pennycook, A. (2008). Translingual English. *Australian Review of Applied Linguistics, 31*(3), 301–9.

Pennycook, A. (2012). *Language and mobility: Unexpected places*. Multilingual Matters.

Perera, N. (2020). "I'm kind of agnostic": Belief discourse by second-generation migrants at the Tamil Saiva temple. *Australian Review of Applied Linguistics, 44*(3), 328–46.

Pérez-Milans, M. (2015). Language and identity in linguistic ethnography. In S. Preece (Ed.), *The Routledge handbook of language and identity* (pp. 1–15). Routledge.

Phillipson, R. (1992). *Linguistic imperialism*. Oxford University Press.

Phillipson, R. (2010). *Linguistic imperialism continued*. Routledge.

Phillipson, R., & Skutnabb-Kangas, T. (1995). Linguistic rights and wrongs. *Applied Linguistics, 16*(4), 483–504.

Piller, I. (2016). *Linguistic diversity and social justice: An introduction to applied sociolinguistics*. Oxford University Press.

Ramjattan, V. A. (2020). Engineered accents: International teaching assistants and their microaggression learning in engineering departments. *Teaching in Higher Education*. https://doi.org/10.1080/13562517.2020.1863353.

Ramjattan, V. A. (2022). Accenting racism in labour migration. *Annual Review of Applied Linguistics, 42*, 87–92. https://doi.org/10.1017/S026719052100143.

Rampton, B., Charalambous, C., & Charalambous, P. (2019). Crossing of a different kind. *Language in Society, 48*(5), 629–55.

Riach, P. A., & Rich, J. (2002). Field experiments of discrimination in the market place. *The Economics Journal, 112*(483), F480–F518.

Rishel, T., & Miller, P. C. (2017). English learners and the risks of suicide. *Journal of Thought, 51*(3–4), 3–21.

Rodgers, R. F., Berry, R., & Franko, D. L. (2018). Eating disorders in ethnic minorities: An update. *Current Psychiatry Reports, 20*(10), 1–11.

Rosa, J. (2016). Standardization, racialization, languagelessness: Raciolinguistic ideologies across communicative contexts. *Journal of Linguistic Anthropology*, *26*(2), 162–83.

Rosa, J., & Flores, N. (2017). Unsettling race and language: Toward a raciolinguistic perspective. *Language in Society*, *46*(5), 621–47.

Ruecker, T., & Ives, L. (2015). White native English speakers needed: The rhetorical construction of privilege in online teacher recruitment spaces. *TESOL Quarterly*, *49*(4), 733–56.

Salhi, K. (2002). Critical imperatives of the French language in the francophone world: Colonial legacy–postcolonial policy. *Current Issues in Language Planning*, *3*(3), 317–45.

Salonga, O. A. (2015). Performing gayness and English in an offshore call center industry. In R. Tupas (Ed.), *Unequal Englishes: The politics of Englishes today* (pp. 130–45). Palgrave Macmillan.

Sayer, P. (2013). Translanguaging, TexMex, and bilingual pedagogy: Emergent bilinguals learning through the vernacular. *TESOL Quarterly*, *47*(1), 63–88.

SBS. (2019). Coroner recommends more support for international students after 27 suicides in six years. https://bit.ly/3SBg0Hu.

Schreiber, B. R. (2015). "I am what I am": Multilingual identity and digital translanguaging. *Language Learning & Technology*, *19*(3), 69–87.

Seals, C. A., & Olsen-Reeder, V. I. (Eds.) (2019). *Embracing multilingualism across educational contexts*. Victoria University Press.

Shachaf, P., & Horowitz, S. (2006). Are virtual reference services colour blind? *Library and Information Science Research*, *28*(4), 501–20.

Shah, A. (2017). Ethnography? Participant observation, a potentially revolutionary praxis. *Hau: Journal of Ethnographic Theory*, *7*(1), 45–59.

Shaw, S., Copland, F., & Snell, J. (2015). An introduction to linguistic ethnography: Interdisciplinary explorations. In J. Snell, S. Shaw, & F. Copland (Eds.), *Linguistic ethnography: Interdisciplinary explorations* (pp. 1–13). Palgrave Macmillan.

Skutnabb-Kangas, T. (2000). *Linguistic genocide in education – or worldwide diversity and human rights*. Lawrence Erlbaum.

Skutnabb-Kangas, T. (2015). Linguicism. In G. Gertz & P. Boudreault (Eds.), *The encyclopedia of applied linguistics* (pp. 1–6). Sage.

Stroud, C. (2001). African mother-tongue programmes and the politics of language: Linguistic citizenship versus linguistic human rights. *Journal of Multilingual and Multicultural Development*, *22*(4), 339–55.

Sultana, S., Dovchin, S., & Pennycook, A. (2015). Transglossic language practices of young adults in Bangladesh and Mongolia. *International Journal of Multilingualism*, *12*(1), 93–108.

Sussman, N. M., & Truong, N. (2011). Body image and eating disorders among immigrants. In V. Preedy, R. Watson, & C. Martin (Eds.), *Handbook of behavior, food and nutrition* (pp. 3241–54). Springer.

Tai, K. W. H., & Li, W. (2021). Constructing playful talk through translanguaging in English medium instruction mathematics classrooms. *Applied Linguistics, 42*(4), 607–40. https://doi.org/10.1093/applin/amaa043.

Takeuchi, J. D. (2022). Code-switching as linguistic microaggression: L2-Japanese and speaker legitimacy. *Multilingua*. https://doi.org/10.1515/multi20210069.

Tankosić, A. (2020). Translingual identity: Perpetual foreigner stereotype of the Eastern-European immigrants in Australia. *Australian Review of Applied Linguistics*, 1–26. https://doi.org/10.1075/aral.20078.tan.

Tankosić, A., & Dovchin, S. (2021). (C)overt linguistic racism: Eastern-European background immigrant women in the Australian workplace. *Ethnicities*, 14687968211005104.

Tankosić, A., & Dovchin, S. (2022). Monglish in post-communist Mongolia. *World Englishes, 41*(1), 38–53.

Tankosić, A., Dryden, S., & Dovchin, S. (2021). The link between linguistic subordination and linguistic inferiority complexes: English as a second language migrants in Australia. *International Journal of Bilingualism, 25*(6), 1782–98.

Tebaldi, C. (2020). "#JeSuisSirCornflakes": Racialization and resemiotization in French nationalist Twitter. *International Journal of the Sociology of Language, 2020*(265), 9–32.

Tenzer, H., Pudelko, M., & Harzing, A. W. (2014). The impact of language barriers on trust formation in multinational teams. *Journal of International Business Studies, 45*(5), 508–35. https://doi.org/10.1057/jibs.2013.64.

Thompson, R. (2006). Bilingual, bicultural and binominal identities: Personal name investment, (bi)cultural identity negotiation and the imagination in the lives of first generation Korean-Americans. *Journal of Language, Identity and Education, 5*(3), 179–208.

Tian, Z., Aghai, L., Sayer, P., et al. (Eds.) (2020). *Envisioning TESOL through a translanguaging lens: Global perspectives.* Springer.

Tomlinson, B. (Ed.) (2011). *Materials development in language teaching.* Cambridge University Press.

Tonin, M. (2018). Back talk. *Library Journal, 143*(1), 16–17.

Tóth, Z. (2010). *Foreign language anxiety and the advanced language learner: A study of Hungarian students of English as a foreign language.* Cambridge Scholars Publishing.

Tse, L. (1998). Ethnic identify formation and its implications for heritage language development. In S. Krashen, L. Tse, & J. McQuillan (Eds.), *Heritage language development* (pp. 15–27). Language Education Associates.

Tupas, R., & Rubdy, R. (2015). Introduction: From world Englishes to unequal Englishes. In R. Tupas (Ed.), *Unequal Englishes* (pp. 1–21). Palgrave Macmillan.

Wang, M. and Dovchin, S. (2022). Why should I not speak my own language (Chinese) in public in America?: Linguistic racism, symbolic violence, and resistance. *TESOL Quarterly.* https://doi.org/10.1002/tesq.3179.

Wee, L. (2005). Intra-language discrimination and linguistic human rights: The case of Singlish. *Applied Linguistics, 26*(1), 48–69.

Wee, L. (2011). *Language without rights.* Oxford University Press.

Zhang, Y. S. D., & Noels, K. A. (2022). 'Call me "Katy" instead of "Yueyun"': English names among Chinese international students in Canada. *Journal of Multilingual and Multicultural Development,* 1–15. https://doi.org/10.1080/01434632.2022.2098304.

Acknowledgements

I would like to thank the editors of Cambridge Elements in Intercultural Communication, Will Baker, Troy McConachy, and Sonia Morán Panero, for their encouragement. Troy, thank you very much for your constant support and feedback! I also wish to thank the anonymous reviewers, who contributed significantly to the final version of this Element. My gratitude goes to Stephanie Dryden and Felicity Knight for their hard work in copy-editing and polishing the final version. I would also like to thank all my research participants and international colleagues around the world. My special gratitude goes to my colleagues, higher degree research students, and friends at Curtin University. Big thanks to my wonderful research team: Ana Tankosić and Stephanie Dryden. This research was supported by Australian Research Council (DE180100118) and the Department of Home Affairs (4-AXFMHKT).

Finally, to my family. Your support has been tremendous in completing this Element.

To my son, Wilson Dring, and my partner, Elliot Gane, I dedicate this Element to you two. You both have patiently tolerated my ups and downs and passionately listened to my points and arguments. To my dad: I enjoy our weekly online chats. To my mom (who is in heaven): I think of you every day. To my sister: you are the best and sweetest.

Cambridge Elements ≡

Intercultural Communication

Will Baker
University of Southampton

Will Baker is Director of the Centre for Global Englishes and an Associate Professor of Applied Linguistics, University of Southampton. His research interests are Intercultural and Transcultural Communication, English as a Lingua Franca, English medium education, Intercultural education and ELT, and he has published and presented internationally in all these areas. Recent publications include: *Intercultural and Transcultural Awareness in Language Teaching* (2022), co-author of *Transcultural Communication through Global Englishes* (2021), co-editor of *The Routledge Handbook of English as a Lingua Franca* (2018). He is also co-editor of the book series 'Developments in English as Lingua Franca'.

Troy McConachy
University of Warwick

Troy McConachy is Associate Professor in Applied Linguistics at the University of Warwick. His work aims to make interdisciplinary connections between the fields of language education, intercultural communication, and social psychology, focusing particularly on the role of metapragmatic awareness in intercultural communication and intercultural learning. He is author of *Developing Intercultural Perspectives on Language Use: Exploring Pragmatics and Culture in Foreign Language Learning* (2018), Editor-in-Chief of the international journal *Intercultural Communication Education*, and co-editor of *Teaching and Learning Second Language Pragmatics for Intercultural Understanding* and *Intercultural Learning and Language Education and Beyond: Evolving Concepts, Perspectives and Practices*.

Sonia Morán Panero
University of Southampton

Sonia Morán Panero is a Lecturer in Applied Linguistics at the University of Southampton. Her academic expertise is on the sociolinguistics of the use and learning of English for transcultural communication purposes. Her work has focused particularly on language ideologies around Spanish and English as global languages, English language policies and education in Spanish-speaking settings and English medium instruction on global education. She has published on these areas through international knowledge dissemination platforms such as ELTJ, JELF, *The Routledge Handbook of English as a Lingua Franca* (2018) and the British Council.

About the Series

This series offers a mixture of key texts and innovative research publications from established and emerging scholars which represent the depth and diversity of current intercultural communication research and suggest new directions for the field.

Cambridge Elements ≡

Intercultural Communication

Elements in the Series

Translingual Discrimination
Sender Dovchin

A full series listing is available at: www.cambridge.org/EIIC